Magic of Nature

Dedicated to those
who are aware of
the power of the mind
and also to those
who are not yet aware of it

Heinz Schott

Magic of Nature

On the Mystery of Healing

With 68 image pages

BoD – Books on Demand

Bibliografische Information der Deutschen Nationalbibliothek:

Die Deutsche Nationalbibliothek verzeichnet diese Publikation in der Deutschen Nationalbibliografie; detaillierte bibliografische Daten sind im Internet über www.dnb.de abrufbar.

Cover photo:
Borkum (North Sea), sunset with roof of the beach pavilion
(H. Schott, Early August 2009)

SCHOTT's NEUE BIBLIOTHEK / 4

© 2018 Heinz Schott
Herstellung und Verlag: BoD – Books on Demand, Norderstedt.

ISBN: 9783746064956

Preface

What does „magic of nature" mean? Which role does it play in the intellectual history of medicine? Starting with the much-debated placebo effect and its relevance for biomedical research and clinical practice, this treatise focuses on diverse historical concepts of the "healing power of nature". This topos was fundamental for natural medicine, life reform movement, suggestive therapy, hypnotism, romantic natural philosophy, and mesmerism. Such a retrospection leads us to the crucial concept of "natural magic" (Latin: *magia naturalis*), which was essential for early modern medicine and natural science. At that time, Nature (Latin: *natura*) was revered as a divine creator of natural things in the service of God, as a mediator of His wisdom for the inquiring humans. So, *Natura* was personified in many ways as a wise woman or magician, mystically adored by alchemists. Just in the 16th century, one can observe a mixture of *Natura* as a sort of *Alma mater* (nourishing mother) of the world and Virgin Mary, the Mother of God. Such an identification of Nature with a divinely venerated woman dates from pre-Christian religious traditions like the Egyptian Isis cult. Finally, proceeding from the mythological hierogamy or "holy marriage", the study addresses Eros and eroticism between the poles of sexual and spiritual life. At the end, it returns to the present age. It reflects critically modern sexology and sexual medicine confronting their biologistic (naturalistic) understanding of human sexuality with certain spiritually guided practices of "sexual magic".

This essay is an outline of my magnum opus *Magie der Natur. Historische Variationen über ein Motiv der Heilkunst*, which may be translated as *Magic of Nature. Historical Variations on a Motif of the Art of Healing* (Schott, 2014). The book has two volumes including 1350 pages and 373 illustrations. Since its publication four years ago, there were only two book reviews so far: One appeared in the renowned newspaper *Frankfurter Allgemeine Zeitung*, the other one in the electronic newsletter of the Austrian Parapsychological Society (*Österreichische Gesellschaft für Parapsychologie und Grenzbereiche der Wissenschaften*). I received no further reactions apart from some very kind personal replies of friends, who had detected my blog (*Magic of Nature*) presenting the complete text without illustrations. I composed the book during five years and was convinced that it would find a vivid resonance. This was an illusion.

Now, when I give an outline in English representing less than one-tenth of the original size, I hope to get more interested responses than before. I am also in search of a publisher or sponsor, who is ready to support a translation of my original opus into English. Perhaps such a person is among the readers. I am sorry for my halting English, being unable to break away from my mother tongue (*Muttersprache*) properly. But I decided to get the job done without support of a professional translator. The supplementary image pages stand for themselves displaying an emblematical subtext.

Bonn (Germany), in January 2018   Heinz Schott

TABLE OF CONTENTS

Chapter One

PLACEBO – THE VEILED IMAGE OF THE TRUE MEDICINE

Paradoxical healing effect

The placebo effect is a logical challenge for the academic medicine: A placebo drug has an effect without containing an effective substance. How can this happen? Objectively ineffective, the placebo drug is nevertheless subjectively effective, which can be objectively assessed. The medical doctrine presupposes that regarding a real or true drug the subjective-psychical effect can be clearly separated from the objective-pharmacological effect. In this way, the placebo effect appears to be just a subjective reaction of the mind taking a fake drug for a real, true one. Insofar it is a sort of a psychological projection, imagination, or even delusion.

The contemporary evidence-based medicine (EBM) has focused on the objectivation of the placebo effect. It developed together with the information technology in the 1990ies. But the so-called randomized controlled trial (RCT) is about 30 years older. The concept of the placebo effect was introduced in medical terminology in the 1950es signaling a novel methodology of clinical research, especially in the field of pharmacology. For the first time, meta-analyses were performed. They showed that roughly one third of the test subjects felt a remarkable recovery of their state of health because of the placebo effect, which was the stronger the more they suffered from anxiousness and stress (Beecher, 1955).

The controlled randomized trial was from now on appreciated as the only scientifically valid form of evidence of the effectiveness of the specific drug therapy. By this procedure the pseudo effectiveness of a placebo should be determined. Why became the placebo problem so popular in medical research of the 1950s, the early after-war epoch? Two circumstances may have contributed to this situation: on the one hand, the growing interest in medico-psychological topics fostered by the intensive reception of the Freudian psychoanalysis in the United States, and, on the other hand, the expanding pharmaceutical industry developing novel drugs, which had to be tested by human experiments.

The introduction of the so-called placebo effect as an explicit concept coincided with the introduction of psychotropic drugs. Naturally, also in former times human experiments were performed to investigate the substantial (real, true) effect of a therapeutic method or drug by statistical methods. But a scientific methodology developed not before the 20th century.

Nocebo like an evil spell

The fact is well-known, that medicinal drugs and medical doctors can harm patients without being consciously aware of it. Then, they apply a special sort of an evil spell. The manner, how a diagnosis is communicated, a prognosis is declared, a drug is applied, or a treatment is performed, is essential and often decisive for the outcome of a medical intervention. So, not only healing processes can be disturbed, but also healthy people made ill. Since the outgoing 19th century the double-edged power of suggestion and auto-suggestion was theoretically described, experimentally investigated, and therapeutically applied. Hereby the "iatrogenic disease" was considered as an object of medical psychology, i.e. the disease introduced by the physician. Regarding the nocebo effect I am less interested in the so-called medical malpractice, but much more in the subtle influence, which destructive attitudes of physicians may exert on their patients making their health condition worse or even provoke it. For example: The palpation of the abdomen in the case of a supposed appendicitis eliciting the specific symptom of a rebound tenderness (Blumberg's sign) may also be felt by persons with a healthy appendix all the more, as the doctor is convinced of a real appendicitis.

Only in the 1990es, "nocebo" was introduced as the counter-term of "placebo". The research on the nocebo effect is still at the beginning. So far, just a fraction of the means for the placebo research was spent for it. But it is for our issue of great interest because one may understand the nocebo effect as an unconscious process of magic, a hidden act of "black magic". That does not mean the rather rare case of a doctor harming his patient deliberately, but the transfer of harmful suggestions mostly unnoticed by the persons involved producing pathogenic effects and sometimes even severe symptoms. This can happen in medical practice as well as in everyday life.

Evidence-based medicine

The concept of *evidence-based medicine* (EBM) emerged in the 1990s. Originally developed in Canada, it was approved in biomedicine all over the world. But one should be aware that already about 20 years earlier the so-called practice guidelines for special therapies in several clinical disciplines were created by experts communicating systematically e. g. in consensus conferences. This approach is considered today as a forerunner of the EBM. But based purely on clinical observation, it could only generate less "evidence" than the EBM with its statistical research methodology.

The EBM came into the picture, when the digitization spread in science and the economization of the health system escalated. It offered medical doctors ostensibly a solution of their economic problems, especially regarding their knowledge about the most cost-effective alternative. The concept of the quality management is closely linked with this economic dimension of the EBM targeting to avoid losses by the inappropriate saving of necessary actions respectively the ineffective or harmful application of remedies. Nevertheless, the advocates of EBM and quality management generally reassure that always the well-being of the patient has to be in the focus and not the cost reduction. The idea of optimizing, essential in mathematics and business economics, tries to use the resources as money-saving and as effective as possible. It belongs to the belief system of the proponents of the EBM that the interests of the patient are as well preserved as the interests of the community of solidarity, so that they would coincide in fact.

Scientific progress

The history of medicine and science is commonly understood as a progressive revealing of the truth. This evolutionary view recognizes only *one* direction of movement: from an earlier to a later, from a more primitive to a higher, from a backward to a developed condition. Often there is the talk of "stages" of progression illustrating science ascending higher and higher. This reminds of Jacob's ladder, a well-known metaphor of the early modern natural philosophy symbolizing the approach to divine truth. Insofar, the secular manner of speaking is oriented towards the former idea of a mental ascent to heavenly wisdom.

At least since the 18th century, historiography favored a popular pattern of thinking, namely that the "development" or "progress" of science and technique would be automatically accompanied with a growing knowledge of the "truth" in regard to natural processes and their relevance for men. But which sense makes the scientific-technical progress in the face of death inevitable for the individual because of biological reasons and for mankind because of cosmological ones? The death problem contradicts the idea of progress and reveals it as an absurdity, a problem, science cannot really handle with.

"Nature" as an object

The term "biomedicine" was only coined at the end of the 20th century. Until then the term "natural scientific medicine" was commonly used, besides "academic", "university", or "school medicine", often understood as synonyms, nevertheless indicating different meanings in a historical perspective. Particularly two traits of this medicine have to be differentiated: on the one hand. the natural scientific objectivation of the healthy and ill organism by the experimental approach, on the other hand, the sophisticated manipulation of the organism by specific technical means. Both approaches merge in medical practice and can hardly be separated. Obviously these traits of the natural scientific medicine fit to the situation in pre-modern times. We may just think of the vivisection of humans by anatomical researchers in Alexandria in the third century A.D. (Staden, 1996) or the discovery of the systemic circulation in the 17th century by animal experimentation (Mani, 1996). But the natural scientific medicine in our present understanding became only established in the second half of the 19th century, when physics, chemistry, and biology became the leading sciences of the academic medicine.

"Disenchantment" of magic

According to Max Weber, an essential factor of the progress due to modern science was the "disenchantment of the world". The progressing "intellectualization and rationalization" would have led to the knowledge or belief, that there were no mysterious, unreckonable forces, that one could rather bring all things under control through calculation: "This means that the world is disenchanted. One need no longer to have recourse to magical means in order to master or implore the spirits, as did the savage, for whom such mysterious powers existed. Technical means and calculations perform the service. This above all is what intellectualization means." (Weber, 1922) Weber's formula can also be employed on the academic medicine: Through disenchantment of the religious and magical healing arts it depends no longer on priests and sorcerers, but is able to provide calculable ("scientific") methods and techniques for rational diagnostics and therapeutics. In fact, such a general formula went along with the natural scientific revolution in medicine refuting resolutely the "occultism" as an obsolete ideology of the past. So, the triumphant natural scientific medicine was celebrated as a glorious process of disenchantment, which was even significant for the implementation of the suggestion doctrine (see Chapter Three).

Placebo therapy

The difficulty of the placebo therapy concerns all fields of medical practice and is especially important for general medicine, psychosomatics, and oncology. What appeared to be credible fifty years ago, raises an ethical dilemma today. On the one hand, the therapeutic target may demand the application of a placebo, on the other hand, this requires that the patient is not informed about it and so may fall a victim to the consciously cheating doctor. So, the compromise formula is to find a layer of information in between the strongest effectivity of the placebo and the most extensive patient information. Therefore, under certain conditions, the placebo therapy in clinical medicine is useful and permitted. But according to its scientific self-image, curative medicine focuses on the application of specifically effective drugs (*verum* preparations) respectively approved interventions. Therefore, medicine practicing exclusively placebo therapy has to be considered unscientific: in the best case as harmless, in the worst case as harmful or even criminal. In the discourse of placebo research, two important realms of pre- or unscientific placebo therapy are identified, which could be compared with an "ocean" of the placebo effect: The historical concepts of pre-modern, non-scientific medicine (like humoral pathology), and the contemporary concepts of alternative medicine (Shapiro, 1960, p. 114).

Chapter Two
HEALING SPRING – NATURE AS A MASS IDOL

Natural medicine movement

When the modern industrial society developed, the so-called civilization diseases were focused by health policy and medicine assuming that those ailments were caused by harmful living conditions. The stressful form of social life in regard to housing, working, and traffic seemed to cause primarily certain diseases in the view of many contemporaries. These conditions were slammed as "unnatural". "Nature" on the other side became the standard for all things, which seemed to be good, beauteous, and healthy.

The critics of civilization and skeptics of progress highlighted the eternal natural laws harmed by the doubtful achievements of civilization. "Nature" became a mass idol. It became the ultimate authority for all social reform movements worshiped by academic societies as well as by popular lay associations. Natural medicine (German: *Naturheilkunde*) and life reform (German: *Lebensreform*) had many appearances, but only *one* great idol: "Nature" (Latin: *natura*). The artistry of the *Jugendstil* (art nouveau) shows this trait most obviously. Also natural sciences, especially biology and medicine, invoked Nature as the unique health-giving source of life, which seemed to be buried more and more by the stupidity of men. Social Darwinism and race hygiene expressed this ideology very clearly. So, the image of the sound, "pure" Nature was opposed to the image of the degenerated civilized man suffering from nervousness and other diseases. On the other hand, Nature symbolized the healing spring per se. "Healing spring" was not meant just metaphorically. Real healing springs have been venerated since antiquity. In the 19th century, they underwent a novel boom linked with the natural medicine movement. Nature seemed to emit its healing power particularly into its element water, and therefore hydrotherapy became a prominent healing method. Especially in ominous spring waters, the magic of nature was supposed to work most effectively.

Divine Nature is the counter-image of the evil, dangerous Nature, where things annihilate each other threatening permanently humankind. The admiring contemplation of Nature on the one hand, and the ambition to rule over it on the other hand, indicate an ambivalence wavering between affectionate respect and brutal aggressiveness. Especially in the 19th century, the period of the technical-industrial revolution, the dialectic between the respect of the "marvels of nature" und the proud of the "victory over nature" developed (Radkau, 1994, p. 292). For some protagonists of the modern natural sciences like the chemist Justus von Liebig life appeared to be a "continuous fight with the natural powers" intending "to destroy ceaselessly" the human existence (ibid.). One conceited cultural history respectively history of civilization mainly as a process of emancipation from the acts of nature, as a successful fight against the dangerous nature. Considering the natural disasters nature was thought to be incalculable and untamable – like the earthquakes of Lisbon (1775) and Messina (1908), or the Tsunamis in the Indian Ocean (2004) and off Japan (2011).

In early modern medical literature, especially in the writings of Paracelsus, the events of the "great world" (macrocosm) were taken for analogous procedures of the "small world" (microcosm), i.e. the human organism. So, certain disorders of the human body were described as "earth quakes" or "fluxes" within the microcosm. But even when the human organism was separated from its cosmological and natural-philosophical context in the course of the modern times, the idea of the dangerous nature persisted. The natural scientific-biological medicine of the 19th century created new strategies by its novel leading disciplines bacteriology and eugenics, fighting the disease as its deadly enemy. The imagery of war in medicine corresponded to the imagery of war common in society influenced by the maxims of nationalism and imperialism at that time.

The "New Man"

The life reform movement was a cultural respectively subcultural response to the upcoming industrial society. It was a sort of defensive reflex against the changed living conditions due to the industrial revolution: urbanization, pauperism, technological change, characteristic for the emergence of the capitalistic class society.

The life reform had diverse ideological roots: It was coined by the ideas of Enlightenment, especially by the theory of Jean Jacques Rousseau claiming man being good by nature, a noble savage. Education should unfold the natural state of its fosterlings. Moreover, it oriented itself towards certain views of the romantic natural philosophy, which thought to understand the original divine language of nature by studying its signs. That stimulated an attitude of mysticism. Its sense of mission came in addition: The life reform movement tended to loosen restricting bonds in everyday life and to free the alleged suppressed, ill, and wretched people guiding them to a new morning and, more or less, to a paradise on earth. Hiking songs of the 19th and 20th centuries, some of them still popular as hits today, reflect the atmosphere of departure. A lot of such songs were still well-known in post-war Germany and sung by young people, as I can remember personally, e.g. *"Im Frühtau zu Berge"* or *"Aus grauer Städte Mauern"*.[1]

Temple of Nature

Two topoi were omnipresent characterizing scientific research as a quasi-religious act similar to a worship. Firstly, the topos of reading in the "Bible of nature" as the other Holy Scripture was very common in the early modern period, and even emerged as a title of the great work on insects by the Dutch naturalist Jan Swammerdam (1738/39; 1752). Secondly, the topos of carrying out research in the "temple of nature" became rather popular about 1800 pointing at the "temple of reason" as well as the "temple of science". So, the veneration of the goddesses Isis, Artemis, or Diana identified with *Natura*, just to mention the most important ones, was not just an act of contemplation, but aimed primarily at the discovery the natural laws unveiling the true nature. The metaphor of the temple was crucial for natural science in the 19th century, as the great didactic poem *The Temple of Nature* by Erasmus Darwin, the grandfather of Charles Darwin, shows. So, the famous French physiologist Claude Bernard called the laboratory the "genuine temple" of science (Bernard, 1865/1961, p. 314).

It is remarkable that all tendencies to replace the traditional religion by a religion of reason and to dissolve the divine instance totally in the realm of Nature could not relinquish religious rituals and their numinous locations. Consequently, the profane "temples" and their inventory were carefully cultivated. In the history of natural science a radical iconoclasm did never happen, the former gods and goddesses were never totally forgotten. At least, they

---

[1] http://www.volksliederarchiv.de/text1168.html (Sept. 11, 2017).

were useful for decoration. So, the herma of the Diana of Ephesus was integrated into the monument of the physicist and physiologist Hermann von Helmholtz, erected in 1899 in the front court of the Humboldt University in Berlin, where it is still there.

Degenerated Nature

There is no genuine consistent ideology of National Socialism. It absorbed very heterogenous directions of thought, and probably this specific mixture made its terrific brisance possible. Three ideological attitudes as stimulating factors should be differentiated: (1) a concept of history claiming a spiritual-cultural *Sonderweg* (special path) of German history; (2) a concept of nature highlighting the biological natural laws as the ultimate authority in the sense of race biology, and (3) an admiration of the technique targeting supremacy and world conquest, which demanded maximal efficiency.

We just focus on the second attitude, the concept of nature. Basically, all the ideas of natural medicine and life reform movement were compatible with national socialistic politics and could more or less coopted. So, the speculations on natural magic blossomed in certain esoteric circles inside and outside medicine. They were very eager to slam scientific intellectualism and cultural "degeneration." Alleged simple truths passed on by the people for hundreds of years in popular medicine were now in great demand. Magic and religion seemed to be of fundamental importance because of their estimation as a specific trait of the German essence. So, Paracelsus was taken for the archetype of the German physician und got the honorable title "Luther of the physicians" (*Lutherus medicorum*), an expression, which had come in vogue since the era of romanticism (Schott, 2007). In this view, Goethe's *Faust* symbolized the German drive for research and conquest and was put on a nationalistic pedestal.

What was the concept of nature in the "Third Reich"? It was expressed by images convenient for mass idols, useful for the propaganda, and strengthening the "social cohesion", a term coined by the psychoanalyst Erich Fromm in 1932. Neither the external machinery of power, nor the rational interests could warrant the functioning of the society according to Fromm: "The libidinous tendencies of men produce so to speak the cohesion [German: *"Kitt"*, putty], without that society could not keep together, and which contribute to the production of the great social ideologies in all cultural spheres." (Fromm, 1932, p. 50, transl. H. S.) In the case of a socioeconomic crisis the traditional social bonds would cease to be „*Kitt*" and become explosive. Certain images had obviously the function of an ideological clamp combining diverse directions of thought. So, natural philosophy, religion, biological racism, and technological enthusiasm could merge. They coined the *"Zeitgeist"*. One could also argue the other way round : The *Zeitgeist* created the images, which had the power to fascinate groups and masses of people. Accordingly, the eminent dissemination of Fidus' (i.e. Hugo Höppener) illustrations in the first half of the 20th century was due to their usability as ideograms delighting his contemporaries.

Pure Nature

The biblical narrative of Paradise, the Fall, and the expulsion from Paradise has been often repeated in a more or less concealed form throughout the history of medicine and science. It was especially appreciated by representatives of the romantic natural philosophy. As an example, one could mention Gotthilf Heinrich Schubert's "The

Symbolism of Dream" (*Die Symbolik des Traumes*) (1814) turning the narrative to a language theory typical of the time. He identified the Fall of Man with the Tower of Babel and the subsequent confusion of tongues. Now, man would be deaf for the sense of God's language and also for the original ("hieroglyphic") language of nature. Therefore, he would be cut off from his own origin. Analogously, the theory constructions of Karl Marx and Sigmund Freud reflect this narrative of man being condemned to live in a non-paradisal environment because of his own guilt. The capitalistic surplus value resulting from the alienated labor, and the neurotic misery resulting from the Oedipus complex fostered by the murder of the primal father, point both to a supposed original healthy state without alienation and neurosis. Such a view implicates automatically the therapeutic question: How can man return to Paradise, understand the language of God again, get totally rid of his neurosis – what Freud thought to be impossible –, or at least reduce his disorders to a convenient extent?

The ecological movement of our time took over the legacy of the *Lebensreform*. It uses the narrative of the Fall and argues consequently: Man took possession of Nature, driven by greed and delight in destruction; and punishment respectively revenge follows sin. So, the German news magazine *Der Spiegel* titled a report on the flood disaster at the Oder 1997: "At the Oder nature takes vengeance for the sins of decades" (*Schlacht an der Oder*, 1997). "Nature strikes simply back", commented an official of the local environment agency. In this context, the river was not only declared as an avenger of the environmental sin, but also as a "fateful river" (*Schicksalsfluss*) deciding fate once again as a curious being, just wanting to observe, how neighbors would get on together. The pattern of such a thinking is evident: Nature offended and harmed by man hits back and revenges his wickedness.

Second Nature

The conceptual history of the "second" or "other nature" (Latin: *secunda* or *altera natura*) can be traced back to the ancient Greek philosophy. The idea was central that nature and education as processes of transformation showed a certain similarity. Education and habituation would produce a sort of nature, namely customs apparently given by nature. Well-known authors used the concept throughout the ages: from Democritus, Aristotle, and Cicero, over Augustin and Thomas Aquinas, Montaigne and Pascal, to the German idealism and the cultural philosophers like Arnold Gehlen. More important for our topic is another perspective: the comparison of nature with art. Since antiquity, art was understood as an imitation of nature, until finally in the Renaissance the idea came to the fore that the art was a second creation and the artist a second god creating a second nature (Funke / Rath, 1984, col. 484). Insofar, the artist and the poet in particular were regarded being made in the image of God. In this sense, Giordano Bruno upgraded the creative power of man in his dialogue *"Lo spaccio della bestia trionfante"* (*The Expulsion of the Triumphant Beast*, 1584). Leibniz named the poet another God (*poeta alter deus*), which became later a slogan of the genius cult in the age of Goethe.

Medical anthropology understood the second nature particularly as a harmful cultural achievement causing illness: It would suppress and weaken the physical vitality (drives, instincts) of man's first nature and produce in this way the "modern disease" (Nietzsche) or "neurosis" (Freud) coming along with the development of culture respectively the process of civilization. Also in the view of social medicine and social pathology the idea of the second nature became important. The social criticism of Karl Marx focused on the "alienated labor" (*entfremdete Arbeit*) in the capitalistic production process generating the fetish character of the consumer world. The objectivity of value ("*Wertgegenständlichkeit*") of the material goods ("*Warenkörper*"), into which "no atom of natural substance would enter", becomes then the second nature of man. So, the real origin, namely the production of the surplus value, remains unknown or unconscious going on "behind the producers' back." (Marx, 1968, p. 599). The capitalistic externalization and pauperization of the working class or proletariat had devastating consequences for health and conduct of life, not least in the form of "civilization" or "lifestyle diseases".

Chapter Three
SUGGESTION – THE MAGIC FORMULA OF DISENCHANTMENT

Salutary Suggestion

When scientific medicine prepared to overcome once for all the legacy of the romantic natural philosophy and its magical implications, the natural or naturopathic medicine (German: *Naturheilkunde*) originated as a great countermovement. It adopted traditional elements of the early modern natural magic and kept them alive. But such elements were also put on the agenda of the academic medicine, often with a new terminology.

It is remarkable that sleep and dream were the starting points for modern psychotherapy and (dynamic) psychiatry. The physician and natural philosopher Gotthilf Heinrich Schubert coined the topos of the "Night Side of Natural Science" (*Nachtseite der Naturwissenschaft*; Schubert, 1808). In his view, magical apparitions had a specific link to night, sleep, dream, and somnambulism. Accordingly, the upcoming natural medicine was also interested in this occult sphere, romantic medical doctors were convinced of. Especially those of them, who wanted to overcome classical mesmerism in favor of a more psychological respectively psycho-physiologic approach focused on the reinterpretation of the sleep. So, the "magnetic" shifted to the "nervous sleep", and the "somnambulistic" state of consciousness was explained to be a "hypnotic" one. So, occult phenomena like clairvoyant dreams, telepathy, or distant healing seemed to be just illusions of the imagination, phantasy products documenting the "power of the mind over the body", as James Braid put it in the 1840es (Braid [1846], 1882).

The concept of suggestion is quite important regarding the "magic of nature". It marks a crucial turn in the history of medicine formulating the paradigm of psychotherapy, psychosomatics, and medical psychology still valid nowadays. Until mid-19th century it was not unusual to deal with alleged occurrences of natural magic and correlating healing methods as real subjects of the natural sciences and medicine, like Carl Gustav Carus did it e.g. in his late writing on "life magnetism" and "magical effects in general" (Carus, 1857). Not later than about 1880, there was a fundamental historicization of this topic. Any natural magic altogether with all possible magical arts was now realized just as a historical fact, i.e. a scientifically obsolete approach. It represented obviously the former superstition, charlatanism, and infatuation. The dividing line between the obsolete past and the promising presence was marked by the concept of suggestion. With its help the entire history of science and culture, which happened *before*, was now viewed as the pre-history of true scientific cognition. The former marvels seemed to be understood and the secrets revealed. So, "suggestion" became the magic formula for medical psychology and in particular psychotherapy including psychoanalysis.

Pathogenic Suggestion

The clinical psychotherapy in the sense of the French internist Hippolyte Bernheim, the founder of the modern suggestion therapy, succeeds, when the hetero-suggestion of the medical doctor exerts a healing effect by means of the auto-suggestion of the ill person. But the contrary can also happen: Certain harmful hetero-suggestions may be taken over by respective auto-suggestions making a healthy person ill or a diseased person still worse. If a medical doctor gives such suggestions, consciously influencing his patient (what would be a criminal act) or unconsciously using them in the course of his treatment, it is likely that he produces "iatrogenic" disorders. Then, he harms his patient and affects him personally as a "nocebo".

According to the classical doctrine of suggestion, the auto-suggestion of the person concerned is lastly decisive for the effect of a hetero-suggestion. Not only the doctor may – unconsciously – apply a sort of harmful spell. The (ill or healthy) person may also harm himself by his or her auto-suggestions. The medical history reveals an astonishing sensibility just for this topic, well-known not only in academic medicine throughout the times. The importance of the placebo and nocebo effect for medical practice can hardly be overestimated.

Hypnosis

The key concept of suggestion originated from the discourse of hypnotism appearing as a therapeutic method and a topic of psychological research in the mid-19th century. It did not claim to be a counterpart to the natural scientific medicine, rather it stressed to be its psychological complement. It is noteworthy that simultaneously to the natural scientific change of medicine in the mid-19th century, hypnotism was established as a new paradigm of medical psychology and psychosomatic medicine. The Scottish surgeon James Braid defined the "nervous sleep" in his groundbreaking writing *"Neurypnology; or, the rationale of nervous sleep considered in relation with animal magnetism"* (Braid, 1843). He laid the first foundation of modern psychotherapy compatible with the upcoming natural scientific medicine. Of course, hypnosis performed in public was for a long time suspected to be dubious and dangerous, provoked by shady show hypnoses onstage as well as spiritistic and parapsychological experiments in the twilight of hidden séances. Nevertheless, hypnotism became the matrix of modern psychotherapy named "dynamic psychiatry" by the Canadian psychiatrist and medical historian Henri F. Ellenberger according to his magnum opus *"The Discovery of the Unconscious"* (Ellenberger, 1970).

The Unconscious

The concept of the unconscious is generally ascribed to the Freudian psychoanalysis and its depth psychological offspring. It was often indisputably reified, when interpreters were not aware that respective explanations are just constructions, "auxiliary constructions" or parables, as Freud put it. So, he said regarding the "psychic apparatus" in his magnum opus "The Interpretation of Dreams", one would need "auxiliary ideas for the first approach to any unknown subject", but must not "take the scaffold for the building".[2] The ahistorical definition of the concept of the unconscious in encyclopedic or textbook articles is apparent, particularly when the so-called topographic model of the psyche (Conscious, Preconscious, Unconscious) is schematically confronted with the so-called structural model (Ego, Id, Super-ego) later on. According to Henri F. Ellenberger, today's historiography of psychiatry and psychoanalysis acknowledges generally that the scientific pre-history of modern depth psychology or "dynamic psychiatry" starts with Franz Anton Mesmer's concept of "animal magnetism". The popular term "discovery of the unconscious" suggests that the unconscious had been previously an unknown subject brought into the light of day due to Sigmund Freud. In this perspective magic, shamanism, and spiritual healing appear then as the earliest evidence of the effectiveness of the unconscious, whereas mesmerism and hypnotism would belong immediately to its historical origin.

---

[2] https://en.wikisource.org/wiki/The_Interpretation_of_Dreams/Chapter_7 (Oct. 2, 2017)

I do not intend to follow up the history of magic in the sense of a Whig historiography maintaining that magic would have been overcome by scientific progress resulting in the psychology of the unconscious. Rather I would like to ask, how far the concept of the unconscious itself includes magical dimensions. Obviously, the tradition of natural magic continues in it, showing surprising cosmological and anthropological aspects. So, one may understand the unconscious as a manifestation of natural philosophy in the form of modern psychology. But I intend less do explain historically the "development" or "evolution" of the unconscious with precedent natural-philosophical theories. Rather, I try to get a new approach to former positions by discussing the actual concept. It is in line with an evolutionary theory of history to deduce the present from the past assuming a certain "evolution", "explication", "differentiation", where later events follow more or less inevitably earlier ones. The concept of contingency or coincidence (*Zufall* in German) contradicts such a causal deduction. In my opinion, it is much more interesting to consider first the strange subject of the past in an unbiased way to question our self-assured certainties. So, the reified concept of the unconscious may be dissolved to a certain extent to regain its historical significance.

Transference

The concept of transference as it is used in medical psychology and psychotherapy was essentially coined by Sigmund Freud. It defines a psychological process of projection. "Transference" and "countertransference" are understood as the crucial means and effectiveness of the doctor-patient-relationship explaining its dynamic according to psychoanalysis. But the conceptual history is more complicated. That is to say, it indicates magical, natural-philosophical, and religious implications making the modern understanding appear in a different light. It is not only about the psychological *projection* from subjective, internal complexes to external objects, which themselves would not be substantially affected by that, but also about psychological *infections* contaminating external objects, e.g. when a human being incorporates a message from another one dominating his or her imagination like a parasite or demon. In such a case of corresponding, both sides become linked and show phenomena, which were attributed to "sympathy" or "rapport" in the era of mesmerism. The early modern concept of "natural magic" understood nature in general as a transmitter of divine powers, which man had gratefully and humbly to accept.

Especially the concept of imagination illustrated the idea of transference: An *imago* (image, picture) is transferred from the environment into the inward organism, e.g. a morbid idea (*idea morbosa*) as Johan Baptista van Helmont phrased it in the 17th century. Such an imagination could radically intervene in the life process, reshaping or even destroying it. In the demonological concept of possession and exorcism, but also in early modern magical medicine, the transfer or "transplantation" of the evil respectively the disease (Latin: *transplantatio morbi*) played an essential role, e.g. the healing of possessed by transfer of the demons to other natural things like animals or plants in particular. All corresponding medical models suppose that a (harming or curing) transfer or transmission only happens, when it has enough power to overcome the specific "resistance". In other words: The transfer of a power originating from an external source or sender will only succeed, when the inward resistance of the receiver can be overcome – or is anyway insignificant. This dynamic is generally effective in disease-causing attacks on the integrity of the organism as well as in therapeutic operations to strengthen the weakened organisms or to remove a "foreign body".

Mass suggestion

The French Revolution, the historic paradigm of mass psychology, had shown, what a crowd of human beings could achieve, which cruelties it was able to perform under certain circumstances. The outcropping terror (French: *terreur*) seizing furiously the mind and stimulating men to commit brutal misdeeds collectively motivated many, mostly conservative scholars to question, how such horrible incidences could happen. The scientific discourse on this problem led to the emergence of modern mass psychology. At the end of the 19th century, bacteriology and hypnotism functioned likewise as explanatory models for "mass hysteria" and collective delusion. Basically, the question was, by which mechanism a crowd of decent people was bound together and become a murderous horde. The formation of a consensually feeling and acting crowd of people is one of the marvels challenging cultural anthropology and social psychology. Most prominent authors like Gustave Le Bon (1895) and Sigmund Freud (1921) used the concepts of hypnotism and suggestion to give an answer. Nowadays, regarding the mass media and the expanding digital world of the internet, the importance of mass suggestion, inducing collective delusions and thereby triggering mass actions or behavior, is still significant.

Spirit and spirits (ghosts)

The concept of the mind respectively spirit (*Geist*) is quite confusing in regard to medical history. It refers on the one hand to the omnipresent divine authority (Holy Spirit) and its corresponding counterpart within the human intellect, on the other hand, there are multiple "spirits" of different quality. This diversity was of great importance for the early modern "natural magic". First of all, the physiological dimension has to be considered: "life spirit" (Latin: *spiritus vitae*) and "nerve spirit" (*spiritus nervosus*) were still common in medical terminology about 1800. They were supposed to be ruling stimulators within the human organism, conducted by the nerve system. The macrocosmic dimension of the spirit belonged to the elementary nature. So, Paracelsus differentiated between four "elementary spirits" (*elementargeister*), which was echoed many times in the history of arts and literature.

Especially romanticists were interested in evil, pathogenic spirits. The "evil magnetic" (*"kakomagnetischen"*) phenomena could be treated by exorcism according to the Swabian doctor and poet Justinus Kerner. But good spirits, guardian angels, spirits of the deceased could encounter some somnambulistic "seeresses", too. In the view of the spiritualist Andrew Jackson Davis, the perverse evils appeared as pests, which had to be fought with support of "Mother Nature". Because of the fact that the "spirit" or the "spirits" during the course of history were ascribed to God, devil, nature, or the human nerve system, they seemed to found a network linking terrestrial and extra-terrestrial things, this world and otherworld, good and evil, microcosm and macrocosm. While the romantic naturalists in the early 19th century wanted to decipher the "hieroglyphic language of nature" (*"Hieroglyphensprache der Natur"*), the spiritualists some decades later were more interested in the otherworld, inaccessible since times out of mind. Now, It should be opened up with the help of so-called „media", which were able to interpret hidden messages of the divine Nature for this world. The contemporary modern means of telecommunication like telegraphy and telephony were used as technological models making the transcendent world of spirits visible and even materialize them. In this regard, the discipline of parapsychology with its natural scientific claim is quite remarkable. It shows a strict endeavor to rationalize the irrational, to catch the volatile spirits by technical means, e. g. photography.

Chapter Four
FLUIDUM – MEDICINE OF SYMPATHY

Electricity and Magnetism

The ability to produce artificial electricity by machines and to catch heavenly electricity by lightning rods symbolized a new age of natural science (*Naturforschung* in German) in the mid-eighteenth century. The electricity hype elicited sensitive commotions in the era of Enlightenment, when electric phenomena were related to und identified with magnetism according to the tradition. So, even in antiquity, the attracting power of the rubbed amber (Greek: *elektron*) seemed to be an equivalent of the virtue of the magnetic iron ore (Greek: *magnetis lithos*). But only at the beginning of the 17th century, electricity and magnetism could be scientifically separated from each other. In his pathbreaking book *"De magnete"* (1600), the English naturalist William Gilbert indicated a method, how to produce a permanent magnet and discussed the "electric power" (Latin: *vis electrica*) as an attractive power evoked by rubbing certain bodies. Finally, in the early 18th century, the construction of two devices accomplished the technical breakthrough. Since about 1730, one could produce relatively simply frictional electricity by an electric machine consisting of rotating glass cylinders with a leather cushion driven by a fly wheel. Some years later, in 1745, the Leiden (respectively Kleistian) jar was invented, which functioned in combination with the electric machine as a capacitor.

"Lightning", "spark", "illumination", "beam" or "shock" described not only the sensitive perception of the artificial electricity, but also symbolized generally the essential idea of the "Enlightenment", in French *Lumières* and in Italian *Illuminismo*. For some naturalists, especially in the sphere of pietism, electricity meant a sort of religious illumination. For the first time, man succeeded in provoking apparently magical, even divine powers of the occult nature. So, they were able to catch divine lightnings from heaven by experimentation with lightning conductors invented by Benjamin Franklin. The historian of religion Ernst Benz characterized this attitude as "theology of electricity" representing the so-called "physicotheology" or "natural theology" (Benz, 1971). Before this background, Franz Anton Mesmer's "discovery" of animal magnetism has to be considered. He was inspired by the idea of natural magic and tried to adapt it to the novel advances of experimental science coined by the Newtonian physics and the phenomena of artificial electricity. With other words: Mesmer intended to study the magic of nature using the technique of "magnetizing" (mesmerizing), and give it the physicians as well as the lay healers as a natural panacea.

Evil Spirits

In the sense of Enlightenment, Mesmer explained possession and exorcism by his theory of animal magnetism, naturalizing those strange phenomena his way, whereas the romantic magnetizers were ambivalent regarding these events. They envisaged demons and developed therefore exorcist techniques, arguing rather psychologically and at the same time pragmatically: When the practice of exorcism and prescribing amulets turned out to be useful, then one should use it. Especially, the Swabian physician and poet Justinus Kerner (1786-1862) gives an impressing example. The demons were taken seriously and at the same time they were ironicized by the romanticists. The world of the spirits, the good as well as the evil ones, appeared as an esthetic Panopticon and spent artists and literates some subject matter for their productions. Demonic and magnetic delusions and confusions were literalized brilliantly by E. T. A. Hoffmann and Edgar Allen Poe among others.

Mesmerism

At first, we take a look at the literary reception of mesmerism in the present medical historiography. In my view it shows two characteristics: On the one hand, mesmerism appears to be a precursor of modern psychotherapy, as its very beginning. So, it is often more or less identified with hypnotism representing the prehistory of modern psychotherapy. On the other hand, its scientific and natural-philosophical rootedness in the occidental history of science and culture is often neglected, in particular its specific continuation of the early modern *magia naturalis*. Mesmeric ideas about 1900 were generally suspect and blamed for propagating "occultism". So, they were excluded from the discourse of academic medicine. Just the most important message of mesmerism, namely the assumption that the "magic of nature" was the key problem for medical theory and practice, most essential for the concept of disease and its therapeutic consequences, was then ignored by the academic medicine. But beyond that, the continuing effects of Mesmer's doctrine became obvious and influenced diversely natural medicine (*Naturheilkunde*), alternative medicine, and esotericism.

Mesmerism was also called "healing magnetism" (*Heilmagnetismus*) in circles of popular or lay medicine, which highlighted its applicability as a universal remedy or panacea. Particularly, the romanticists stylized it as a traditional healing method, which had been always used by ordinary people like shepherds and rural men. It is remarkable, how strongly mesmerism fascinated medical doctors as well as (lay) healers at that time. When from mid-19th century on mesmerism together with some other healing methods had to quit the field in favor of natural scientific medicine, it migrated to the booming lay respectively alternative medicine. It experienced together with natural medicine a considerable renaissance. The advice literature on mesmerism and hypnotism – terms mostly mentioned in the same breath and often used synonymously – circulated very impressively in different classes of population and imposed especially the adherers of the natural medicine movement (Schott, 1985). Some of the pamphlets and manuals for domestic use had a large circulation.

As an example, one may cite Gustav Albert Geßmann, an Austrian officer and occultist, who authored many popular non-fiction books from the 1880es to the 1920es, among them one titled "Magnetism and Hypnotism" (Geßmann, 1987). The basic idea of mesmerism was simple: Because allegedly all bodies including the human one seemed to be immersed in a so-called ocean-like *fluidum*, which could be introduced into the human organism via the nerves, it was a challenge for the healing art to pool the *fluidum* and transfer it to the patient. There were different methods to accomplish it according to the relevant literature: magnetic strokes (French: *passes*) with the palms over the surface of the body, treatment around the "magnetic tub" (French: *baquet*) in a group, and other "magnetic" manipulations e.g. drinking "magnetized water". Magnetizing was frequently combined with other healing methods supposedly intensifying them, like homeopathy, phrenology, or galvanism. Those procedures tended less to produce the "magnetic sleep" or somnambulism, rather they should amplify the healing effect of the respective concept, e.g. cranioscopy (in the sense of phrenology).

First of all, we have to stress the importance of Mesmer's original healing concept, which is often misunderstood even by professional historians of science and medicine, confusing – similar to Mesmer's contemporaries – animal magnetism, mineral magnetism, and electricity. So, one reads in an academic biography on the botanist Christian Gottfried Nees von Esenbeck, an outstanding expert of the mesmeric literature of the day, that Mesmer produced electricity by his *baquet* and would have transferred the so-called *fluidum* obtained by electricity into the body of the patient (Bohley, 2003, p. 53). So, it would have been electrotherapeutics, which was applied as magnetic therapy under a false label!

Somnambulism, Dream, Ecstasy

In 1808, the German medical doctor and natural philosopher Gotthilf Heinrich Schubert published a sort of manifesto resonating strongly with his contemporaries inspired by romanticism: *„Ansichten von der Nachtseite der Naturwissenschaft"* (Views from the night [or: dark] side of science). It was fundamentally coined by mesmeric ideas circulating at that time. The "dark side" announced a new approach to the secrets of nature according to the new awareness of the "magic" of nature, which had been detected by scientific research. So, some phenomena of the human condition came to the fore associated with "night": especially sleep, dream, somnambulism, and ecstatic states of consciousness. Above all, the scholars were interested in the perceptions, sensations, visions, i.e. in those manifestations becoming perceptible, visible, audible in the darkness of the night. Hereby, one assumed, it would be possible to catch the very nature, which remained hidden during the day. Only when the daily noise becomes silent and the bright light of the day shrinks from the darkness at night, the subtle messages of nature could be perceived. For this, the sleep was a precondition, not the insensible deep sleep but, the spontaneous dream sleep or artificially induced "magnetic sleep". Mesmerism provided seemingly a reliable method, how natural scientists and doctors at that time could not only evoke the magnetic sleep in patients, but also produce it experimentally in test subjects, what often coincided. Probably, the "magic of nature" has been never investigated more intensively and more seriously than in the romantic-mesmeric milieu of the early 19th century.

Somnambulistic "Seeresses"

In the view of the doctors inspired by romantic natural philosophy, the magic of nature related basically to the inner nature of man, as it was allegedly revealed by somnambulistic patients or by persons in an altered state of consciousness. Therefore, somnambulism – "artificially" evoked or "spontaneously" emerging – became an object of investigation and a means of therapy. The somnambulist was understood as an intermediary of the hidden divine nature, a sort of religious prophet. Accordingly, some doctors adored their patients, especially the younger female ones. One of the most famous case histories happened in the early 19th century: The "Seeress of Prevorst", authored by Justinus Kerner, a public medical officer and romantic poet. The magic of nature allegedly emerged according to the mesmeric doctor in the experiencing, which his severely ill patient communicated. Kerner venerated her almost like a saint. He admired Mesmer, the founder of animal magnetism, to the core, but never encountered him personally. Decades after Mesmer's death in 1815, he transferred the very few pieces of his *Nachlass* from Meersburg to his residence in Weinsberg. Until today, they are preserved in the *Kernerhaus*, now a museum. Moreover, Kerner also wrote the first Mesmer biography (Kerner, 1956).

Sympathy

The concept of sympathy (Greek: *sympatheía*, Latin: *consensus*) emerged in medical terminology for the first time in the Hippocratic writing "On diet" (*De diaitia*), indicating the functional interaction of all parts of the human body (Hippocrates, 1962, pp. 225-261). In the second century A.D., the Greek physician Galen defined "sympathy" in the context of humoral pathology as the disorder of an organ caused by the disorder of another one. As early as in antiquity, this physiological understanding of sympathy was contrasted by a cosmic-biological one: The stoics stressed the idea of a unifying power, which they called *pneuma*, connecting every single body with the cosmos, a huge organism animated by the "world soul" (German: *Weltseele*). The idea of an interaction or correspondence between microcosm and macrocosm lived on and became important for early modern medical alchemy and magic. "Natural magic" with its corresponding magical arts, then known as "sympathetic magic" (German: *Sympathiezauber*) in academic and popular medicine, flourished even in the age of Enlightenment, despite of the progressing knowledge of the natural sciences at that time. The concept of "animal magnetism" with its *fluidum* theory gives us an illustrious example (see below).

About 1800, the concept of sympathy mixed natural-philosophical, mystical-religious, (neuro-)physiological, psychosomatic, and depth psychological elements apart from its adaptation in literary and artistic works. Only the concepts of natural scientific medicine becoming dominant in the second half of the 19th century, like the reflex doctrine e. g., made the traditional key concept of sympathy disappear. Nevertheless, the idea of sympathy was often taken up again using it as a counter project to criticize the deeply felt fragmentation of the modern world. In today's ordinary language "sympathy" means only the emotional affection of one person to another one, whereas all the other dimensions of meaning have nearly totally vanished.

Fluidum

Mesmerism revealed a comprehensive imagery of light beam phenomena known from the tradition of mysticism and natural magic. They were interesting for medical doctors and natural philosophers for practical as well as philosophical reasons. So, light beams radiating from certain parts of the body – especially eyes, palms, and fingertips – could reportedly be seen by numerous people. Particularly, their magical power would become apparent by actions at a distance. The visualized *fluidum* impressed sensuously as the healing power of nature, conventionally illustrated with light beams, in the first place with sun beams. The *fluidum* came into sight as a marvelous natural power, an "animated gravity" (*gravitas animalis*) according to Mesmer's dissertation, nearly ten years before he established his concept of "animal magnetism" about 1775.

Such a visualization of the healing power of nature as a radiating beaming was rather popular in the realm of mesmerism and natural philosophy about 1800. But even after their golden age in the early 19th century, concurrent phenomena were observed and described again and again. It may be mentioned casually that the light as a symbol of truth is crucial for philosophical metaphorology in the sense of Hans Blumenberg (2001). *Fluidum* is a colorful Latin term. Some similar terms in everyday language are derived from it, like "fluid" (German: *Flüssigkeit*), "flood" (German: *Flut*) or "flow" (German: *Fluss*). Moreover, the Latin term *effluvium* (plural: *effluvia*) (German: *Ausfluss*) belongs to this linguistic complex, which should explain the magical action at a distance.

Chapter Five
Magia naturalis – Nature as a Female Magician

Divine light

In Renaissance and early modern times, the upcoming natural philosophy, inspired especially by Neoplatonism, identified by no means God with nature. Insofar, they did not advocate pantheism. Rather, one could name it "theological naturalism": Nature made an appearance as a voice and conductor of divine messages and powers. The triadic hierarchy top down: God – Nature – Man was principally set to instruct man about the main direction of his activity. He should ascend from earth to divine wisdom, the eternal origin of light, through exploring the secrets of nature. So, it is no surprise that the metaphor of Jacob's ladder played an important role in the early modern discourse of natural philosophy. It symbolized the targeted rise of man, enabled by his education and self-education, relieving him from misery on earth and bestial compulsions. Ascending this cosmic ladder implied the pathway to an *unio mystica*, which should be achieved through the right way of natural science taking Nature seriously as a school master and following its (her) footsteps. So, we come across another metaphor obligatory for natural philosophers, respective natural scientists (so-called "curious" people, *Naturforscher* in German): Nature as a (female) leader, guide, master. But the divine source of light would not always be passed on through nature, quasi broken down by this medium. It could also directly light up appearing immediately before the eyes of man, moving and glaring him similarly to the effect of the sun, the main celestial body.

As far as *Natura* appeared as a mediator or medium of divine reve-lation, it (she) represented the salvation per se: healing power and source of life for all creatures and especially for man. On the other hand, there were the doctrines of the evil originating from Mani-chaeism and Gnosticism, which demonized the material world as a place of evil in general. In this view, all kinds of natural things were tinged with the evil, quasi permeated by the devil and his potency.

"Natural magic" in Renaissance and early modern period disem-powered the realm of evil: It was still ubiquitous with regard to demonology and black magic, but it was no longer almighty. One could defend oneself. In the case of an attack. one was able to fight against the evil power expelling it from the sphere of life. Magic and religious rituals applying amulets and exorcism display this specific sort of healing art. In this perspective, black magic on the other hand formed an alliance with the dark, evil side of nature and con-verted good into evil. "Woe to those who call evil good and good evil, who put darkness for light and light for darkness, who put bit-ter for sweet and sweet for bitter!"[3] The biblical word hits the core of black magical procedures and their operators converting good into evil, light into darkness. To put light for darkness meant to send out disease-causing "dark" beams of the evil. In the history of medicine, particularly in the tradition of popular medicine, black magic as a harming spell, a malefaction (Latin: *maleficium*) played an important role provoking disease, suffering, and death. The col-or "black" points to the evil source, the "kernel of the brute" (*des Pudels Kern*) according to Goethe's *"Faust"*.

---

[3] http://biblehub.com/isaiah/5-20.htm (Nov. 8, 2017).

Imagination

In the view of early modern natural philosophers, nature used a magical mechanism to influence man, literally impressing its (her) seal upon him. They named it imagination (Latin: *imaginatio,* German: *Einbildung*). This process was fancied very vividly and concretely as an image from outside entering the organism, unfolding there its coining effects, and becoming apparent through certain alterations or deformations of the body. Thus, the imagination always involved an impression. *Imaginatio* was a key concept of the doctrine of Paracelsus combining indistinguishably psychosomatic, demonological, parasitological, and infectiological aspects. The concept of natural magic (*magia naturalis*) assumed, that the imagination started with an external image, which was internalized, then developed as an internalized image its own dynamics, causing thereby eventually diseases and malformations.

In the outgoing 18th century, this paradigm changed under the influence of the Enlightenment: Now, imagination meant the projection of an internal image on the external world without a corresponding object there. In other words: Introjection was reinterpreted psychologically as projection. So, imagination stood for illusion, delusion, spleen, fancy. So, the "imaginary disease" popularized by Molière's classical play "The Imaginary Invalid" was taken as a consequence of the weakness of character or of an overexcited nerve system, and not as a disease originating from internalized images from outside. This may be exemplified by the doctrine of the "tooth worm" and its refutation. In the early 18th century, it was accepted in general, that "tooth worms" would cause toothaches and tooth decay. For the medical authorities, this was just a fact. So, the Parisian professor of medicine Nicolas Andry recommended, like other medical doctors, to fumigate the teeth with henbane.

Then, one would "soon observe the worms coming off out of the mouth, attracted to the air by this fume." (Schäffer, 1757, p. 10 seq.; transl. H. S.) The German theologian and natural scientist Jacob Christian Schäffer, who authored numerous studies on natural history, refuted this worm doctrine through a self-experiment "to sound the death knell of the whole worm story" (ibid., p. 26). He explained in his information pamphlet published in 1757: The alleged tooth worms did not emanate from the teeth, but from the burnt henbane. Everybody could convince himself of this fact. One should take "a fiery iron, put it on a purely polished stone, throw henbane seed on the fiery iron, and cover it rapidly with a funnel; so, one perceives certainly a lot of wormlike corpuscles beneath the funnel, but will also be convinced of the fraud of supposed miraculous cures." (Ibid., p. 42; transl. H. S.) The internal worm turned out to be an artifact falsely identified with an object of the external world. In the imagination, it was projected from inward to outward, although it really came from outside: So, it became just an "imaginary" worm.

Effluvia: Magical outflow

In early modern folk medicine and especially veterinary medicine, magical practices were quite usual. They were mostly criminalized as pagan remnants by Christian authorities. So, the Merseburg incantations (*Zaubersprüche*) document their pagan origin. In a 16th century tract on the "superstitious legends", it is apodictically stated that only God could bless, and somebody, who would bless by himself, would make himself equal to God, just as Lucifer did (Spretter, 1543, Aiiij; p. 5). Magical methods of treatment were generally blamed as diabolic, especially when they turned out to be effective. So, when one bandaged a chair leg in the case of a leg fracture of a domestic animal (sheep, hound) and let the animal untreated. Often, the animal was helped in this way, but that would have done "the devil to cheat man". If the animal could not be helped by natural means, "the devil is then the doctor." (Ibid., p. 5 seq.)

The proponents of natural magic had to solve a big epistemological problem: They hat to uncover the "supernatural" respectively "diabolic" phenomena as natural ones, which could be rationally comprehended and deliberately manipulated. In particular, the long-distance effect of the "supernatural" processes had to be explained rationally through the mechanisms and techniques of the transfer of powers, in medicine most notably the transfer of healing powers or diseases. Insofar, the concept of transference, defined by psychotherapy and psychoanalysis, has a great historical scope. It is rooted in the thinking of "natural magic". There, one used the traditional term *"effluvia"* meaning the magical outflow (German: *Ausdünstungen*) to explain and illustrate the mysterious, invisible transfer. Already in antiquity, Galen's physiology used this concept explicating the doctrine of sympathy. Thereby, the naturalness of magic should be declared, since the "outflows" (the literal translation of *effluvia*) originated from natural things themselves, not from supernatural powers like demons or the devil.

Signatures

One theorem of the natural magic claimed that Nature would draw or sign its (her) creatures. So, their shape, consistence, and color would reveal their essence, especially their hidden healing power; e.g. the red color of a stone would indicate its hemostatic effect, or the testicle-like root tubers of orchids would expose their virility-stimulating and fertilizing virtue. But nature also designed man, his body shape, face, skull. At the end of the Middle Ages, *Natura* was also depicted as a female blacksmith fabricating man in her forge. However, the devil could also have a hand in it. Regarding misfortune and disease, natural scientists and medical doctors were interested in the stigmata of the evil explaining them sometimes according to demonology as devil's work. They had the duty to recognize the signs of nature and to interpret them workmanlike for the benefit of mankind. The signatures of nature should be taken as seriously as the letters of the Holy Scripture.

In the following we focus on those signatures in particular, which relate to man himself marked by nature. Especially the physiognomics of Giambattista Della Porta (1535-1615) and the craniology of Franz Joseph Gall (1758-1828) had a great impact on medical anthropology later on. Their aftermaths are noticeable until today. The signature doctrine underwent most dubious modifications within the context of race biology. So, criminal anthropology about 1900 and later on claimed the physiognomic approach for its purpose, which was rather incorrect in the perspective of today's history of science. After which model did Nature design man according to Della Porta's early modern physiognomics? There is a simple answer: after the animal. The individual human physiognomy was brought into the line with personality typologies identifying the traits of character of man with those of animal species resembling them: E.g., a cunning person turned out to be a fox, an avaricious one a raven. 200 years later, Gall applied a more sophisticated methodology based on the results of his abundant investigations in the field of comparative brain anatomy.

Which ambition had natural-philosophical research in the Early Modern Age? The alchemical drug production in the tradition of Paracelsianism gives a paradigm. This concept is also named "iatrochemistry", "chemiatry", or "chemical medicine". The respective procedures targeted a very subtle, pure, rather spiritual medicament beyond the impure matter, the so-called *Arcanum*. Therefore, the alchemists tried to sperate the polluting material, the "feces" (*Schlacken* after Paracelsus) from the effective remedy through their laboratory work. In other words: The natural things should be spiritualized as completely as possible through a systematic handling. Moreover, the early modern alchemy was always about the education, the spiritualization of the alchemist himself. He was deeply involved in the process of purification, which he celebrated in his laboratory. The idea was obvious that he could become himself a sort of an *Arcanum*, when he practiced alchemy in a serious way. Paracelsus stressed the "virtue" (*virtus*) of the physician in his writing *"Paragranum"*, pointing to the alchemically acquired self-refinement, which is not just a congenital virtue given by nature. The refinement or spiritualization mentioned above proceeded bottom up: from earth to heaven, from matter to spirit. The magician should ascend Jacob's ladder – from the earthly dark to the divine light. The metaphor of Jacob's ladder emerged in the discourse of early modern natural philosophers. The divine light (Latin: *lumen dei*) was not only believed to be the source of all knowledge, but also of the very healing power. Who got there, had attained the *Arcanum* – objectively as a producer of medical drugs, subjectively as a mystically enlightened adept having experienced the divine origin of the magic of nature. *Arcanum* means according to Zedler's *"Universal-Lexicon"*: "a secret, immaterial [*uncörperliche*], and immortal matter [*Sache*], which can only be recognized by humans through experience. And it is the virtue [*Krafft*] of a thing [*Sache*], thousand times more effective than the thing itself." (Zedler, 1732: col. 1182; transl. H. S.). There were different realms of *Arcana*: "secrets of nature (*arcana naturae*), secrets of God (*arcana Dei*) and secrets of the authorities (*arcana imperii*)." (Jütte, 2011, p. 11 seq.) *Secretum* and *occultum* were pretty much used synonymously. They all together expressed a paradox: They indicated besides the hidden contents their secrecy as well as their detection.

"Chymical Wedding"

Ascending Jacob's ladder signified a purification and spiritualization on the way to the *Arcanum* as mentioned above. Insofar, the way of the alchemical work led to a sort of self-realization in the sense of "individuation" described by C. G. Jung. Simultaneously, it implied the approach and unification with the divine wisdom and had therefore a mystic feature (*unio mystica*). For it revolved around a combination, fusion, merging (*coniugatio, coniunctio*), a marriage (*coniugium*). Just the alchemical symbolic focused on the idea of a "marriage" illustrating e.g. the alloy of different metals. So, the natural-philosophical eroticism was formed, which implied the idea of a "holy marriage", often depicted in book illustrations, especially in emblematic tracts. Alchemy, magic, and kabala were closely interconnected in the thinking of Paracelsian scholars. In this way, the imaginary brotherhood of the Rosicrucians were inspired by the impact of that thinking and built on its impressive imagery.

Chapter Six
NATURA – EQUIVALENT OF MARY

Goddess *Natura*

Two characterizations of Nature were of great importance: *Natura* as a Holy Scripture, which should be read and deciphered and the secret language of which should be understood; and *Natura* as a divine female, the veil of which was only permitted to raise with utmost gentleness and empathy. Both views can hardly be separated from each other. It was a central ambition of natural magic (*magia naturalis*) to get on to the "secrets of nature" (Eamon, 1957). Nature was an authority at a higher level. One would not only admire its (her) magical art. On the one hand, one was challenged to analyze and to investigate it scientifically, on the other hand, one tended to imitate and to complete her. The upcoming early modern science academies were committed to this approach. The Italian scholar Giambattista Della Porta from Naples published his most important work *"Magia naturalis"* first in 1558 and founded in 1560 one of the earliest natural scientific academies in Europe, namely the *Academia Secretorum Naturae* (*Accademia dei Segreti*) (Eamon, 1957, pp. 194-233). It was dedicated exclusively to the investigation of nature and affiliated only someone, "who could present an until now unknown secret in the field of medicine or the mechanical arts". (Gronemeyer, 2004, p. 87; transl. H. S.) "Encyclopedias of secrets" were written, and the natural science considered itself explicitly as a hunt (ibid., pp. 273-285). In the end, they had the task to explain the natural mysteries. The Italian physician and universalist Gerolamo Cardano tried to make these mysteries more understandable through his concept of "subtlety" (Latin: *subtilitas*). The topos of the veiled nature became a popular image motif of iconography and emblematic. *Natura* emerged as a woman of different shape and outfit. The Bible story of God's interdiction to eat the fruits of the tree of knowledge (Gen. 2,17) corresponded the Greek legend of Plutarch recorded later in numerous versions. According to that, it was forbidden to raise the veil of the veiled statue of Isis in Sais (Egypt), as dubious or even wicked natural scientist were tempted to do.

Just in the Early Modern Age, there was an ambivalent attitude towards the efforts of natural science. On the one hand, its aggressive execution was forbidden and it should be humbly performed. On the other hand, science attacked Nature directly, e.g. through anatomy or mining. Because God would hide nature, natural science (*curiositas, Naturforschung*) seemed to be a damnable act. The Christian apologist and church father Lactantius had pointed out, that God generated Adam as the last creature to impede that he could gain knowledge of the creative act. *„In confirmation of this, the popular image of the goddess Natura implied that nature covers herself with a veil in order to hide her secrets from mortals."* (Eamon, 1954, p. 59 seq.) The secrets of divine nature should be concealed. It is remarkable indeed, that *Natura* is generally overlooked in the historiography of religion and not even mentioned in relevant handbooks like that of Eliade and Culianu (1995). Whereas the images of female deities like Sophia and Mary were investigated again and again in Jewish studies and theology, they were mostly ignored in historiography of science and medicine. It is a crucial question, whether certain ideas of *Natura* became noticeable in the early kabala of the 11th and 12th centuries leading over to the natural philosophy and natural science later on, especially when one focuses on Mary and "Schechina" in the way of the judaicist Peter Schäfer (2002).

Devil, witches, and evil spirits

The common ground of evil, be it the realm of devil, the actions of witches, or suggestions of evil spirits, was "artificiality" (German: *Unnatur*): the attacks of obfuscating powers darkening the "light of nature" or even quenching it completely. In the thought of the early modern natural philosophy it was quite clear: Everything was evil, what prevented man from following *Natura*. This weighed for physicians and natural scientist as well as for other professional groups and concerned savants and lay persons likewise. Paracelsus used hefty words in his polemics against contemporary authorities disdaining nature. In this perspective, diseases and malformations were viewed as the consequence of a deviate lifestyle: E.g, the perverse sexual intercourse like "sodomy" would generate monsters. But diseases and disorders could also originate from a harmful spell imposed from outside. So, the male impotence (erectile dysfunction) was classic example for the impact of witchcraft. It was correspondingly interpreted in the *Malleus maleficarum* (The Hammer of Witches; first published in 1486 in Speyer), the most important manual of inquisition. This document only reflected, what was common sense at that time anyway. There is a sourced survey with case histories showing the magical explanations of impotence over more than six centuries up to 1450 (Rider, 2006).

The sin against God became particularly apparent as a violation of the alleged laws of nature. This had consequences for the humans, who had incurred guilt: They got literally a brand, became stigmatized. The stigmata of evil played an important role in the history of medical semiotics: from the physiognomics in the 16th and 17th centuries to the physical anthropology in the 19th and 20th centuries, from the psychiatric criminal anthropology to certain esoteric character doctrines. All of those theories argued that the violation of the per se healthy nature would be punished with disease and misery. Accordingly, the witches as allies of devil would poison the human heart and soul. Evil spirits, e.g. originating from a bad constellation of the stars, would mislead man. I skip here the witch hunt, which has been scientifically studied in detail. I only stress the ideological moment of the "unnatural" (deviate; in German: *Unnatur*) as the counterpart of the goddess *Natura*.

Controversial images of women

Throughout the history of occidental medicine, women were thought to be inferior to men. There were two basic theories put forward in ancient medicine. On the one hand, the Hippocratic doctrine of the "wandering womb" (Greek: *hystera*), which would wander through the female body like an animal and produce diverse disorders associated with the classical disease picture of "hysteria". On the other hand, according to the ancient humeral pathology (the doctrine of the four qualities), women were cold and wet and therefore weaker and more prone to illness than men with their hot and dry temper. So, analogue correlations were predetermined: Women belonged to earth, moon, and night, whereas men were linked with heaven, sun, and day. Lastly, women represented the darkness, the evil, and the diabolic, whereas men were associated with the light, the good thing, and the divine. This dualism corresponding to the Gnostic and partially the Christian worldview maintained opposed genders and constructed a fundamental dichotomy, a contradictory value judgement: Women are physically weaker and morally worse than men. So, the gender role was fixed as an apparently natural law: Women had to adapt a passive, serving role as matrons, men an active, conquering role in the life outdoors. Despite of powerful feminist and social reform movements, this cliché was predominant until the second half of the 20th century.

Modern feminism in its various forms fought and fights against the consequences of such ideologically fixed clichés in different social fields like cultural life, politics, economy, and law. We focus just on the historical analyses. Special studies on the correlation of body and gender (Mixa et al., eds., 1996) show two characteristics: (1) They assume – at least implicitly – the equality of sexes. The gold standard of this assumption is the social status of men, from which the discrimination of women is deduced; (2) they ignore usually pre-modern views derived from mythology, religion, and natural philosophy, which may stimulate alternative explaining models.

The labor-law related demand for women's equality is of great importance in the public sphere nowadays. Consequently, certain questions become crucial like „Will women ever get to earn as much as men?" or "Will a woman ever become president?" (Fausto-Sterling, 1992) So, one claims to stop the discrimination against women in regard to career choice, income, or command structure in companies. The supposed suppression of women is not only a topic in the public discourse. Moreover, it is the basis for a new scientific discipline: the gender studies. But it is widely ignored that women's alleged inferiority and real suppression was openly deplored by prominent authors in the past. Some of them even stated emphatically the superiority of the "female sex" in every respect, among them the German polymath Agrippa von Nettesheim (1529/1670).

Mary, the Mother of God

Christ the Redeemer performed miraculous healings according to the New Testament (*Christus medicus*). He became the leading figure in medical thinking, especially in monastic medicine (Fichtner, 1982; Neumann, 1996). The four Gospels report, how Jesus cured lame and blind people among others just by his pure presence or physical contact. What is described here, belongs to the core of Christian tradition. It escapes from the historiographical or psychological access and has to be interpreted theologically. Jesus performed his exorcism on those, whose disease was understood as a manifestation of possession: "For Jesus had said to him, Come out of the man, you unclean spirit. [...] Now on the mountain side there was a great herd of pigs getting their food. And they [the devils] said to him, Send us into the pigs, so that we may go into them. And he let them do it. And the unclean spirits came out and went into the pigs; and the herd went rushing down a sharp slope into the sea".[4] From this time on, healing became a Christian mission to follow and imitate Christ. So, the *imitatio Christi* became the center of the religious art of healing in the Christian Occident for centuries.

It was occasionally pointed to the fact that the figure of *Christus medicus* stood in the tradition of the ancient healing gods following in the steps of Asclepius in particular. But in regard to our topic, Mary, the Mother of God, is even more important, attaining a preeminent impact on the Christian care of the sick. Mary was adored as a divine mediatress advocating for poor and helpless people towards God. Extent and intensity of her adoration exceeded that of the saints by far. She was especially worshiped by the fine arts and popular devotion and invoked in diverse forms for any reason. Her popularity lasts uninterrupted until today. It is fundamental for the identity of the Roman Catholic Church (Grün, 2006). But Mary was not only a counterpart of *Natura*: Both deities be-

---

[4] https://www.biblestudytools.com/bbe/mark/5.html (Nov. 18, 2017)

came merged and were personified as a mixed female figure in the early modern medicine and natural science.

Mary – *Natura*

In the High Middle Ages, the goddess *Natura* was first mentioned in the writings of the cathedral school of Chartres. But then, the relationship to the Mother of God was not explicitly pointed out. For dogmatic reasons, this would not have been possible. But to whom, "who is able to get into the spirit of these writings, it is an 'apparent secret' which 'Ikonia', the power of the imagination, can unveil", stated the writer and anthroposophist Wilhelm Rath (1983, p. 76; transl. H. S.).

In regard to Mary-*Natura*, there were two reverse perspectives in particular prominent in the Renaissance fine arts: On the on hand, the divine Mary got human traits, and, on the other hand, divine qualities were attributed to human women. Something similar happened with the figure of *Natura*: It expressed divine wisdom and represented the Queen of Heaven above this world; at the same time the women of this world could appear as the incarnation of divine nature. In general, historiography assigns these circumstances to two different spheres: Mary belongs to the religious sphere, *Natura* to the natural-philosophical respectively scientific one. In this way, the fascinating momentum gets lost: the personifying formation of a female mixed person blending three images into each other and thus producing a mélange of varieties: the image of (1) the earthly-human woman, (2) Nature (*Natura*), and (3) the Mother of God.

Literary scholars assume that the humanist approach of Alanus, who had viewed Nature as a positive authority, was dismissed by his (German) successors in favor of a Christian religious conception. So, a scholar stated: "When Mary is found, *Natura* totally vanishes." (Rudolf Krayer, quot. from Krewitt, 1990, p. 33; tranl. H. S.) But the history of science shows quite another situation: *Natura* comes proudly and self-consciously into the picture – often equipped with certain attributes of Mary. Although the historiography of religion has worked out the importance of Mary for Christian theology ("Mariology"), it did not realize its impact on the European natural philosophy, which stimulated early modern natural science. (Eliade/Culianu, 1995, pp. 228-230). Insofar, the separation of Mary and *Natura* in the history of ideas should be overcome synoptically to a certain extent.

Matrix, motherly Nature

The creativeness of *Natura* was mainly visualized as a wise woman, a nourishing mother, and in the last consequence as a uterus or *matrix*. One should have in mind that the German medical literature still in the 18th century used "mother" (*Mutter*) synonymously with uterus (*Gebärmutter*), thus speaking of "mother's diseases" (*Mutterkrankheiten*). Still in the early 19th century, "hysteria" was considered as a disorder of the uterus (*Mutterkrankheit, Mutterplage, Mutterbeschwerde*) (Siebold, 1821, p. 417). Paracelsus and Jakob Böhme, the famous theosophist inspired by Paracelsus, often mentioned the term *"matrix"* associating it with Mary, the Mother of God, who served the Holy Spirit as a *matrix*. It is primarily an organ of conception, fertilization. According to the quality of the power, which fertilizes the *matrix*, it generates good or bad fruits. In the eyes of the early modern scholars, the conception, out of which all life comes out, was a mystery and Mary's Immaculate Conception by far the greatest one. Regarding Paracelsus and Jakob Böhme, the concept of *matrix* implied cosmic dimensions and particularly a correlation of divine and natural acting. The magic of nature turned out to be the mystery of the *matrix*. Such a merging of natural-philosophical and theological ideas has been a challenge for modern interpreters. Often, they tended to avoid it and separated therefore both dimensions. This is obviously the case with the reception of the writings of Paracelsus. In the early 20th century, the leading editor Karl Sudhoff divided the complete work into two sections: the medical and natural-philosophical writings as opposed to the theological and religio-philosophical ones.

Luna, the Moon

The cosmological gender problems revolved around sun and moon, the two dominant celestial bodies. The light and warm sun symbolized manhood and spirituality, the darker and cooler moon womanhood and materiality. So, already in ancient times, the sun was equated with father god and the moon with mother goddess. Day and night were characterized correspondingly: day as an active period of creation, night as a passive period of recreation. The moon as a goddess (e.g. as "queen of the night") was associated two other female deities, similarly personified: *Natura* and Mary. In terms of the history of ideas, the assignment of *Natura* to the night and the earthly life was crucial: It (she) was thus the next superior authority for the earthly life and the human being in particular, who lived in the so-called "sublunary" world. This world was seen in quite a different light according to the respective point of view. In the daytime, the nightshades vanished under the sunlight. So, on one side, one claimed that these were anyway negligible. On the other side, one was convinced, that just those things becoming invisible in daylight, would be the really important ones.

Here, we are confronted with a basic controversy in the history of ideas, already laid out in the doctrines of Plato and Aristotle and culminating in the dispute between the advocates of Enlightenment and romanticism about 1800. It was crucial that the romanticists interpreted the psychic life cosmologically. The professor of medicine Dietrich Georg Kieser from Jena showed this in a drawing. He assumed the complementary duality of the "day and night side" (*Tag- und Nachtseite*) of the psychic life. He attributed all psychic phenomena to his model. Regarding the dream, it was plausible to correlate the "unconscious" with the night side, which was in the view of contemporary medicine equivalent to the vegetative or autonomous nerve system.

Chapter Seven

Eros – Spell of Love between Sexuality and Mysticism

Love and Mysticism

In the view of conceptual history, three terms are generally to differentiate: *Agape*, *Eros*, and *Sex*. According to the Israeli historian of religion Moshe Idel, *Agape* is a concept of the unselfish love indicating a spiritual attraction, *Eros* would name a complex of feelings originating from ontological constructs and behavior patterns within a certain culture, and *Sex* would be the somatic satisfaction of an erotic impulse (Idel, 2009, pp. 23-25). Such a conceptual definition conforms with the classical tripartite division of the human being into body, soul, and mind or spirit. It underlies also Aristotle's doctrine of soul in his writing *"De anima"* differentiating between its vegetative, sensitive, and intellectual faculties. This triad was often used in the modern discourse to get a suitable anthropological frame, especially in regard to medicine. So, the German writer and philosopher Joseph Görres located the "mental" (*das Seelische*) in the middle between the "mind above" (*Geist oben*) and the "life below" (*Leben unten*), where the spiritual and the vital spheres would be knotted (Görres, 1836-1842, vol. 3, p. 321). But such a model is problematic: It postulates demarcations, which may be abolished under certain circumstances. This becomes nowhere more evident than through mystical and sexual magical practices. Gian Lorenzo Bernini's famous sculpture "The Ecstasy of Saint Teresa" in the church *Santa Maria della Vittoria* in Rome, completed in 1652, sets an illustrious example. Facial expression and posture were sometimes interpreted as signs of an "orgasm". If one takes her reported mystical experiences seriously: Who may really separate *Agape*, *Eros*, and *Sex*?

In this chapter, the terms "eros" and "love" are considered only insofar, as they refer to the idea of natural magic and natural curing in particular. Sigmund Freud's definition of Eros as the "life instinct" (*Lebenstrieb*) opposed to the "death instinct" (*Todestrieb*) addressed also the cosmological dimension of the relation between life and death. In contrast to almost all of his epigones, Freud recognized the natural-philosophical and anthropological implications of the death problem. With his concept of the "nirvana principle", he introduced even religio-philosophical aspects into the biologically coined anthropology of his time. But this essay does not intend an exegesis of the Freudian doctrine. Rather it tries to investigate the meaning of love as far as it comes into focus of medical history. So, we are confronted with certain problems like God's love and the healing power of nature as preconditions of medicine, love as a healing factor in the doctor-patient-relationship, love causing and expressing a disease ("love sickness"), sexuality as the biological base of "normal" and "pathologic" love life and its importance for sexual medicine, and finally the spiritual power of love mastering sexual desire. There was an interesting discussion in more or less esoteric circles to sublimate the animal sexuality by specific (seemingly utopian) practices of "sexual magic" counteracting the biologistic understanding of sexuality.

Eros in its meaning of divine love (*Agape*) was a popular topic of philosophical reflection and artistic creation. Eros was always a central theme in medicine and natural science, too. God's love towards his creatures and man's love towards God correlated and interacted in the early modern view. This was crucial for medical treatment as well as for natural science in general. In this perspective, therapy and research could only be successful, when they were inspired by Eros. Particularly, the mysticism was tinged more or less erotically. Paracelsus fostered the idea, that the doctor should devote himself to his patient with divine love in purity and chastity. Eros was regularly associated with the victory of truth and freedom. It was described as "inner light" or "fire" by medical doctors and naturalists. So far, the medical significance of Eros was highlighted in early modern medicine. But often, one starts the historical narrative with the 19th century and ignores decisive key concepts originating from the Early Modern Age and concerning "unscientific" concepts like mesmerism for example.

Sexuality

The term "sexuality" was coined first about 1700, when the "sexuality of plants" was investigated (Camerarius, 1694). Before it was introduced into the medical terminology in the 19th century, one spoke of "natural drives" or "natural instincts" differentiating between God-ordained and deviate, sinful ones. Already in the early modern period, the frame for the modern classification of normal versus pathological sexual life was given. Normality was in line with the God-given "nature", and since the 19th century, it was increasingly reasoned with "physiology" deduced from alleged natural (biological) laws. The idea of degeneration and the civilization criticism based on race biology stimulated a definite statement of the find-de-siècle medical anthropology, which spread: The civilization would make sick, being itself a disease.

Nietzsche and Freud argued in this perspective. The former identified the suppression of the physiological vitality by the "ascetic priests" as the origin of the "modern disease" in general. The latter blamed the suppression of the sexual drive through cultural interdiction for the "neuroses" concerning all humans. Both approaches did not define disease as a pathological anomaly of a healthy normality, but stated that all people would be more or less sick and their symptoms would only gradually differ from each other. That attitude was very popular in the "era of nervousness" (Radkau, 1998). The early modern dichotomy of natural instincts (pleasing to God) and perverse (sinful) ones of lust argued that the morbid condition would be the consequence of an aberration of the right way. That became the basis for the model of deviance later on. The criticism of civilization and culture about 1900 blamed the crookedness of a degenerate and simultaneously degenerating civilization respectively culture following a fundamental lapse: the violation of the iron natural laws. On might this name the unconscious doctrine of original sin of modern biology and medicine. It is obvious at first sight, that it would be problematic to ascribe, in accordance with Thomas Kuhn's "paradigm shift", the doctrine of original sin to the pre-modern and the doctrine of deviance to the modern period. In fact, in the intellectual history of medicine, both concepts run not only parallel, but are often inextricably linked with each other. The concept of disease was coined by this ideological melange. What this means for the concept of sexuality has to be shown.

Holy Marriage

The hierogamy (Greek: *hierós gámos*), also named heavenly or holy marriage, is a fundamental element of the testimonia of mythology and mysticism, hermetism and kabbalah, alchemy and natural philosophy. It relates to the divine or sacred marriage producing the *unio mystica* and imagnined as a sort of copulation of deities among themselves, deities and humans, or humans among themselves. Insofar nature was viewed as divine, also the natural mysticism (German: *Naturmystik*) could be understood as a holy marriage. In the history of science and medicine, such experiences of mergence with natural things were often decisive for scholars to achieve scientific knowledge and theory constructions. No other topic of the intellectual and cultural history is so tempting than the holy marriage to impose the contemporary biologically and psychologically coined image of man on historical testimonia. Nowadays, the holy marriage is biologized, when it is viewed as a sexual act projected into the cosmic, and it is psychologized, when it is explained as an inner-psychic process of maturation or "individuation" after C. G. Jung. The US-American psychiatrist Edward F. Edinger followed Jung's psychologizing of the alchemical symbolism to get an "objective basis" for dreams and other productions of the unconscious (Edinger, 1985: Preface). He tried to class the *"psychic facts based on the method of Jung".* So, he identified the "individuation" with the seven steps of the alchemical transformation culminating in the *"coniunctio".* The biological as well as the psychological understanding correspond to or complement one another. The former recognizes the alchemical symbolism as suppressed sexuality, the latter as spiritual, mental maturation. Both of them press their object into the framework of their respective doctrine. The topic of the holy marriage stimulates speculations in many ways. So, the sociologist Gerburg Treusch-Dieter (1997) interpreted (rather incomprehensibly) the holy marriage as a marriage of the dead (*Totenhochzeit*) and the holy bride as a "dead bride" (*Totenbraut*).

It is mostly ignored that the topic of the holy marriage was also important in medical history. At first, it implied the *coitus*, the coming together, the becoming complete of separate, complementary beings accompanied by voluptuousness and delight. Then, this copulation could eventually generate new life, a human or divine child. But the holy marriage could also aim at the embodiment of health and healing. It released healing powers, created according to the alchemical assumption the philosopher's stone, the quintessence (*quinta essentia*), the marvelous panacea. In the Christian-Occidental tradition, "love" was appreciated as the master-key of medicine, from Jesus Christ to Paracelsus. The commandment of brotherly love was primarily not an abstract moral demand, but rather a request to devote oneself to miserably sick fellow men and to mobilize all the healing powers of nature. The medical ethics of Paracelsus aimed at such a therapeutic mobilization through love. In view of the diverse concepts of medicine, one realizes that the doctor-patient-relation always implies a certain erotic-religious component based on the traditional idea of the holy marriage, however mostly unvoiced. That is not surprising, because every interpersonal encounter and communication is subversively fed by such an idea of bodily as well as mental union. Insofar, the encounter of doctor and patient is just a special case of interpersonal communication.

Love Sickness

In medical history, there are a lot of terms to characterize "love sickness", in particular regarding the authorities of the Arab medicine like Rhazes and Avicenna (Schott, 1993, p. 79). Love as such was often conceived as a sort of sympathetic disease. The term *folie à deux*, common in psychiatry, demonstrates this estimation of love as "delusion of two". Sigmund Freud's reflection on the psychological relationship of "being in love and hypnosis", the latter equaling a "mass formation of two", and his concept of "transference love" (*Übertragungsliebe*) reveal the psychopathological side of love as an interpersonal relationship (Freud, 1921, p. 126; Freud, 1915). Love seemed to be dubious because of its smooth transition to "love delusion" (*Liebeswahn*). It was difficult for psychiatrists to draw definitely the line between normal and pathological love behaviour. Love blew up the individual being of one's own, the rationality related to a single person, or the functionality restricted to *one* organism solely. The phenomena of the mesmeric *"rapport"* showed forms of mental erotic unions of individuals. Besides the conception of love as a disease per se, there has been always the idea in medical history, that one could heal through love in which variation whatsoever, through mental or bodily forms of love: from prayers over charitable care to therapeutic sexual contact. We allude to this topic of love practices here only briefly and will come back to it in the last section of this chapter. In the view of contemporary biomedicine, "love sickness" is no longer recognized as a specific disease. Despite this, one can notice a certain sensibility in today's medicine and psychology, when e.g. the term *"broken heart syndrome"* is discussed in the professional literature.[5]

Sexual Medicine

Only in the 20th century, the terms "sexual science" and "sexual medicine" were coined. Naturally, medicine reflected sexuality and its disorders at all times, although not using the term. Nowhere else in medicine, the image of man and the concept of disease appears as vividly as here. Even though contemporary sexual medicine also claims the culture-bound constructions of sex referring to cultural and social history, it follows mainly the biomedical thought and completes it with sociological and psychological aspects. So, it advocates a "bio-psycho-social model of sex", which was first developed within psychosomatic medicine (Beier/Bosinski/Loewit, 2008, p. 30). The radically altered patterns of sexual life throughout history and their respective scientific and social assessments are

---

[5] http://en.wikipedia.org/wiki/Broken_heart (Dec.1, 2017).

obvious. This may be demonstrated for example by comparing the "construction of masturbation" or the "construction of the female sexuality" at the end of the 19th century with the situation about 100 years later. Masturbation changed from "self-pollution", which was thought most dangerous in every respect, to "self-satisfaction", which is meanwhile recognized as completely benign or even in a way healthy. The female sexuality turned from the obligatory performance of the coitus with the husband to a variety of sexual behavior including extramarital or homosexual intercourse. One may think, that the "constructions" of today would mean a real progress of human sexual life according to scientific knowledge, a successful "removal of taboos of the sexual sphere" (Kaden, 1980; transl. H. S.). Nevertheless, one should cast doubt on current doctrines of sexual science and medicine, which try to define standards of a successful sexual life.

Sexual Revolution

The term "sexual revolution" is generally connected with the introduction of birth control pill and the student movement of the 1960s. Sexual morality changed its perspective radically. Former attitudes were criticized and questioned as anti-pleasure and pathogenic, involving masturbation, pre-marital intercourse, and socalled sexual perversions, i.e. sexual practices "against nature" like homosexuality in particular. About 1900, the originating sexology took up such topics, whereby sexual theories, inspired by the upcoming Freudian psychoanalysis, got lots of exposure. Certain social critics, influenced by the Marxist interpretation of history, equated the ruling capitalism with sexual suppression and the political revolution with sexual emancipation. Respective ideas originated at the end of the 19th century, when the workers' movement adopted essential targets of the life reform movement for its purposes. Focusing on the modern situation, one has to realize that there were also earlier sexual revolutions, when social turmoil resulted in far reaching changes of sexual behavior. Exemplarily, one may remind the transition from the Middle Ages to the modern times, when spreading epidemics like plague and syphilis caused huge social and cultural changes of life style including the sphere of sexuality. In the corresponding chapter of the elaborate two-volume work *Magie der Natur* in German (Schott, 2014: vol. 2, pp. 447-467), mainly the situation of the 20th century is considered. There, the alleged sexual revolutions are critically reflected. It is remarkable to what extent biologism and naturalism dominated the discourse in life sciences then. But in certain alternative social movements inspired by philosophical, esoteric, or religious ideas, sexuality was viewed in a different light. In some circles it was linked with natural philosophy, natural magic, and esoteric conceptions, as we see in the following. But even when such theories and practices seem to be strange and freaky sometimes, they may imply a truthful critic of a nonreflective brutal sex behavior, generally named "sexism". Alternative conceptions of Eros and sexuality may be stimulating to analyze and criticize the contemporary shortcuts of unrefined sexual practices, which produce very often psychical and physical misery.

Erotic Magic

Today, sexuality seems to be free from taboos in two ways. Firstly, man is understood as an instinct being biologically comprehensible, completely pressed hard by his or her sex drive. Secondly, sexuality is used as a stage for public performances, where one is able to act out his or her needs unconcealed in public. So, two dimensions of

Eros are marginalized: firstly, the power of the mind, seemingly strictly cut off from the sexual sphere, being not able to influence or rule it; and secondly, the individual awareness of the unique erotic experience. Scientific medicine frames sexuality biologically, allocating it to the area of the autonomic nervous system, which would work involuntarily beyond the human intellectual life. Accordingly, the individual experience of sexuality disappears from the scientific evaluations, which consider mainly statistical compilations like the frequency of intercourse. However, the early modern natural magic implied very erotic moments, especially in its alchemical modification as mentioned in the previous chapter. The former natural philosopher adoring *Natura* as a foster mother (*alma mater*), or the conjunction of sun and moon respectively gold and silver depicted as a couple in love, are illustrious examples. The sensual erotic approach to divine nature (German: *Gottnatur*) happened most intensively through the mystical unification (*unio mystica*). In particular beginning with ancient Indian religious doctrines, a tradition of sexual magic (*magia sexualis*) developed aiming at the experiencing of a cosmic unification through certain sexual practices. Here, among other methods, the semen retention played an important role.

It is fascinating to observe, how "magical" sexual practices were preached and even put into action at the same time, when the biologistic thought dominated the discourse of the life sciences on sexuality. An esoteric method of sexual intercourse was *Karezza*, a technique of self-controlled sex life, formulated by Alice B. Stockham, a gynecologist and obstetrician from Chicago about 1900. Intercourse should be performed in subtle harmony of both partners avoiding the orgasmic climax and ejaculation. But the *Karezza* method played only a minor role in the life reform movement about 1900, although sexology as an academic topic flourished then more and more. In the history of ideas, natural magic (*magia naturalis*) and sexual magic (*magia sexualis*) are closely interconnected. The latter can be understood as the most intensive level of the former. In this perspective, sexuality may offer a way to experience the holy marriage in one's own body to a certain extent, as a sort of *unio mystica.* Opposite to the dominating teaching of a biologically fixed sexuality, we are here confronted with an alternative idea: a sexual life ruled by a mental acting, a spiritual behavior, which liberates and delights according to former promotors of "sexual magic". Just in this sexual sphere, the balancing act between charlatanism, abuse, and self-conceit on the one hand, and religious delusion, infatuation, and mental disease on the other hand, is quite difficult and rather dangerous. When faced with the sexual misery as a human fate and misfortune, which has not disappeared after all "sexual revolutions", this act of balance may appear nevertheless appealing, as a vision of a concrete utopia.

Epilogue

In the view of historiography, "magic" covers an extensive universe of discourse. The transitions to cross areas like belles-lettres, esotericism, and parapsychology are fluent. The attraction of historical or fantasy novels dealing with magical subjects is due to the ineradicable longing for the marvelousness and the chance to experience it by a specific exercise or mindset. Nowadays, the term "magic" provokes rather different associations: harmless variety entertainment convenient for children's birthday parties or festive evenings; dangerous rituals as it is exercised in satanic sects; erudite endeavors of a Faustian bargain to use the powers of nature for human purposes; parapsychological or paramedical methods to investigate extrasensory perception or telepathic action at a distance and also to apply them therapeutically.

In any case, "magic" displays a counterworld transcending our everyday life and pointing frequently at its "beyond". Magicians of today like their colleagues in former times lead their audience to believe the reality of the phenomena, they can produce for fun. Then, magic turns out to be a technical trick. Satanic cults perform their obscure rituals with an exquisite outfit in an adequate ambience: magic as a black tinted performance, where one can hardy distinguish between drollery and solemnity. The aesthetic consideration of magical phenomena historicizes them und put them in an acceptable distance of the viewers: magic as cultural heritage, which has left deep traces in our collective memory. And lastly many scientists deal with border areas of medicine and psychology to clarify magically appearing phenomena like telepathy or spiritual healing: magic as an object of science, which has to be explored. Finally, we should mention a group of magicians appearing on the scene as healers or clairvoyants, which are mostly taken by the academic medicine for charlatans or fraudsters. So, magic may become a professional field, a service on the esoteric ("alternative") health market.

Of course, I do not adhere to one of these views. But at the same time, I cannot present another definition or concept of magic. I just refute the reduction of "magic" to a narrow perspective ignoring or excluding other ones. I suppose that only an open-minded attitude regarding other perceptions may lead to novel ("scientific") knowledge. So, I plead for a sort of synchronous awareness. Magic is not only related to past events of the history of science and culture, but can also be observed up to the present day. Magic art is based on a sophisticated trick technique. But nevertheless, there are charismatic persons producing phenomena, which seem to be "magical" without using technical tricks. Is the general contempt of magic today to understand as the hybris of a world, which is fascinated, bewitched by its own scientific-technical progress, blocking the critical self-reflection of men living in it?

Bibliography

Agrippa von Nettesheim, Cornelius: *Declamatio de nobilitate et praecellentia foeminei sexus* (*Declamation on the Nobility and Preeminence of the Female Sex*, 1529). Edition with English translation, London 1670.

Beecher, Henry K.: The powerful placebo. *JAMA* 159 (1955), pp. 1602-1606.

Beier, Klaus M./Hartmut A. G. Bosinski/Kurt Loewit: *Sexualmedizin. Grundlagen und Praxis*, vol. 2, München; Jena, 2005.

Benz, Ernst: *Theologie der Elektrizität. Zur Begegnung und Auseinandersetzung von Theologie und Naturwissenschaft im 17. Und 18. Jahrhundert.* Mainz; Wiesbaden, 1971.

Bernard, Claude: *Einführung in das Studium der experimentellen Medizin* (French original edition: Paris, 1865). Leipzig, 1961 (Sudhoffs Klassiker der Medizin; vol. 35).

Blumenberg, Hans: Licht als Metapher der Wahrheit. Im Vorfeld der philosophischen Begriffsbildung [1957]. In: Hans Blumenberg: *Ästhetische und metaphorologische Schriften*. Frankfurt am Main, 2001, pp. 139-171.

Braid, James: *Neurypnology; or, the rationale of nervous sleep considered in realtion with animal magnetism*. London, 1843.

Braid, James: *Die Macht des Geistes über den Körper. Eine experimentelle Untersuchung der vom Baron Reihenbach und Anderen einem „neuen imponderabeln" Agens zugeschriebenen Erscheinungen.* [1846]. In: Der Hypnotismus. Ausgewählte Schriften von J. Braid. Ed. by W. Preyer. Berlin, 1882, pp. 1-37.

Camerarius Rudolf Jacob [Rudolphus Jacobus] : *De sexu plantarum epistola.* Tübingen, 1694.

Carus, Carl Gustav: *Ueber Lebensmagnetismus und über die magischen Wirkungen überhaupt.* Leipzig, 1857.

Eamon, William: *Science and the Secrets of Nature. Books of secrets in medieval and early modern culture*. Princeton, N. J., 1954.

Edinger, Edward F.: *Anatomy of the Psyche. Alchemical Symbolism in Psychotherapy.* La Salle, Illinois, 1985.

Eliade, Mircea / Ioan P. Culianu: *Handbuch der Religionen.* Unter Mitwirkung von H. S. Wieser. Frankfurt am Main, 1995.

Ellenberger, Henri F.: *The discovery of the unconscious. The history and evolution of dynamic psychiatry.* New York, 1970.

Fausto-Sterling, Anne: *Myths of Gender. Biological theories about women and men.* 2nd ed. New York, 1992.

Freud, Sigmund: Bemerkungen über die Übertragungsliebe [1915], in: S. Freud: *Gesammelte Werke*, vol. 10, pp. 306-321.

Freud, Sigmund: *Massenpsychologie und Ich-Analyse.* Leipzig; Wien; Zürich, 1921.

Fromm, Erich: Über Methoden und Aufgaben einer analytischen Sozialpsychologie. In: *Zeitschrift für Sozialforschung* 1 (1932), pp. 28-65

Funke, G. / N. Rath: Natur, zweite [encyclopedia entry]. *Historisches Wörterbuch der Philosophie*, vol. 6. Basel; Stuttgart, 1984, cols. 484-494.

Geßmann, Gustav Wilhelm: *Magnetismus Und Hypnotismus. Eine Darstellung dieses Gebietes mit besonderer Berücksichtigung der Beziehungen zwischen dem mineralischen Magnetismus und dem sogenannten thierischen Magnetismus oder Hypnotismus.* Wien; Pest; Leipzig, 1887.

Görres, Joseph: *Die christliche Mystik.* Regensburg. 4 vols. Landshut, 1836-1842: vol. 3 (1840).

Gronemeyer, Nicole: *Optische Magie. Zur Geschichte der visuellen Medien in der Frühen Neuzeit.* Bielefeld, 2004.

Grün, Anselm: *Bilder von Maria: Erlöster Mensch - Mütterlicher Gott - Urbild des Glaubens.* Stuttgart, 2006.

Hippokrates: Schriften. Die Anfänge der abendländischen Medizin. Ed. by Hans Diller. Hamburg, 1962 (Griechische Literatur, vol. 4).

Idel, Moshe*: Kabbala und Eros.* Frankfurt am Main; Leipzig, 2009. [English original edition „*Kabbalah and Eros",* 2005]

Jütte, Daniel: *Das Zeitalter des Geheimnisses. Juden, Christen und die Ökonomie des Geheimen (1400-1800).* Göttingen, 2011.

Kaden, Rudolf (Ed.): *Allgemeine Pathologie der Sexualfunktionen. Störungen der Reproduktion und der Kohabitation.* Köln, 1980: „Einleitung", pp. 15-17.

Krewitt, Ulrich: Natura, artes, virtutes und Inkarnation. Zum ‚Anticlaudian' Alans von Lille in mittelhochdeutschen Texten, in: *Dialog. Festschrift für Siegfried Grosse.* Ed. by Gert Rickheit and Sigurd Wichter, Tübingen, 1990: pp. 25-42.

Le Bon, Gustave: *Psychologie des foules.* Paris, 1895.

Mani, Nikolaus: Experimentelle Medizin im 17. Jahrhundert. William Harvey entdeckt den Blutkreislauf. Gaspare Aselli findet die Darmlymphgefäße. In: *Meilensteine der Medizin.* Ed. by Heinz Schott. Dortmund, 1996, pp. 207-213.

Marx, Karl: *Ökonomisch-philosophische Manuskripte aus dem Jahre 1844*. In: Karl Marx / Friedrich Engels: Werke. Ergänzungsband. Erster Teil. Berlin, 1968, pp. 465-588.

Modersohn, Mechthild: „Hic loquitur Natura"- Natur als Künstlerin. Ein „Renaissancemotiv" im Spätmittelalter? In: *Idea. Jahrbuch der Hamburger Kunsthalle*. München: Prestel, 1991, pp. 91-102.

Kerner, Justinus: *Franz Anton Mesmer aus Schwaben, Entdecker des thierischen Magnetismus. Erinnerungen an denselben, nebst Nachrichten von den letzten Jahren seines Lebens in Meersburg am Bodensee*. Frankfurt, 1856.

Mixa, Elisabeth/Elisabeth Malleier/Marianne Springer-Kremser/Ingvild Birkhan: *Körper – Geschlecht – Geschichte. Historische und aktuelle Debatten in der Medizin*. Innsbruck, Wien, 1996.

Radkau, Joachim: Natur als Fata Morgana? Naturideale in der Technikgeschichte. In: *Zum Naturbegriff der Gegenwart. Kongressdokumentation zum Projekt „Natur im Kopf"*, vol. 2. Stuttgart-Bad Cannstatt, 1994, pp. 281-310.

Radkau, Joachim: *Das Zeitalter der Nervosität. Deutschland zwischen Bismarck und Hitler*. München, 1998.

Rath, Wilhelm: Einleitung [introdution] to Alanus ab Insulis: *Der Anticlaudian oder Die Bücher von der Himmlischen Erschaffung des neuen Menschen*. 2nd Ed. Stuttgart, 1983: pp. 15-92.

Rider, Catharine: *Magic and Impotence in the Middle Ages*. New York: Oxford University Press, 2006.

Schäfer, Peter: *Mirror of his Beauty. Feminine images of God from the Bible to the Early Kabbalah*. Princeton; Oxford, 2002.

Schäffer, Jakob Christian: *Die eingebildeten Würmer in Zähnen. Nebst dem vermeynthlichen Hülfsmittel wieder dieselben*. Regensburg, 1757.

Schlacht an der Oder. [...] Ein Experte: „Die Natur schlägt zurück." *Der Spiegel* 51 (1997), pp. 22-30.

Schott, Heinz: Bibliographie: Der Mesmerismus im Schrifttum des 20. Jahrhunderts (1900-1984). In: *Franz Anton Mesmer und die Geschichte des Mesmerismus. Beiträge zum Internationalen Wissenschaftlichen Symposion [...] 1984 in Meersburg*. Ed. by Heinz Schott: Stuttgart, 1985, pp. 253-271.

Schott, Heinz: *Die Chronik der Medizin*. Dortmund, 1993.

Schott, Heinz: *Magie der Natur. Historische Variationen über ein Motiv der Heilkunst*. 2 vols. Aachen, 2014.

Schubert, Gotthilf Heinrich: *Ansichten von der Nachtseite der Naturwissenschaft.* Dresden, 1808.

Schubert, Gotthilf Heinrich: *Die Symbolik des Traumes.* Bamberg, 1814.

Siebold, Adam Elias von: *Handbuch zur Erkenntniß und Heilung der Frauenzimmerkrankheit.* 1st vol., 2nd ed. Frankfurt am Main, 1821.

Johannes Spretter: *Ein Kurzter Bericht, was von den Abgötterischen Sägen vn[d] Beschwerden zuhalten, wie der etlich volbracht, vnnd das die ein Zaberey, auch greüwel vor Gott dem Herren seind.* Basel, 1543.

Staden, Heinrich von: Alexandrien als das Zentrum der medizinischen Forschung. Herophilos und die frühe Menschenanatomie. In: *Meilensteine der Medizin.* Ed. by Heinz Schott. Dortmund, 1996, pp. 67-73.

Swammerdam, Jan: *Bybel der Natuure [...].* 2 vols. Leiden, 1737/38.

Swammerdam, Jan: *Bibel der Natur: worinnen die Insekten in gewisse Classen vertheilt, sorgfältig beschreiben, zergliedert, in saubere Kupferstichen vorgestellt [...].* Leipzig, 1752.

Treusch-Dieter, Gerburg: *Die Heilige Hochzeit. Studien zur Totenbraut.* Pfaffenweiler, 1997.

Weber, Max: *Wissenschaft als Beruf.* Vortrag (1922). Online: http://www.textlog.de/weber_wissen_beruf.html (Jan. 8, 2018).

Zedler, Johann Heinrich: *Grosses vollständiges Universal-Lexicon.* Vol. 2. Halle; Leipzig, 1732.

SUPPLEMENTARY IMAGES

With back references to the running text

Placebo

The alleged first depiction of the "placebo"

„Een Placebo": Painted plate by Pieter Breughel the Elder, between 1558 and 1560.

Source: https://www.pinterest.de/pin/422494008775211269/ (6/10/2017)

From a series of plates presenting Flemish proverbs. The Dutch inscription means: „I am a placebo and disposed to keep up my coat everywhere towards the wind [i.e. to float with the tide]".

▷ Chap. 1: Paradoxical healing effect ◁

Workers' movement and natural healing movement

Naturfreunde (friends of nature) in favor of workers' movement

Im Abonnement fl. 1.— jährlich.
Für Mitglieder frei. Einzelne Nummern 10 kr.

Redaction u. Administration
Wien, XVI/₇ Hasnerstrasse 56.

Mittheilungen des Touristen-Vereines „Die Naturfreunde" in Wien.

Nr. 1.   15. Juli 1897.   I. Jahrg.

"Der Naturfreund", title page of the first edition of the transactions of the tourist club *"Die Naturfreunde"* (The Friends of Nature) in Vienna, 1887.

A hiker in the mountains welcomes the uprising sun, symbol of a better life in future, often used in the workers' movement. It praised nature as a source of vitality and a antidot against the tortures of capitalism suppressing the needs of a healthy life.

▷ Chap. 2: Natural medicine movement ◁

Sun adoration

A basic attitude of the life reformers

"Light Prayer" (above left) (1910); "Praying Fellow" (above right) (1906); "Sun Adorers" (about 1910) by Fidus (i.e. Hugo Höppener, 1868-1948), the creator of very popular illustrations of the life reform movement.

▷ Chap. 2: The "New Man" ◁

Personified Healing Power of Nature

A Woman Advertising for a Naturopathic Institute

Postcard (1905); from A. Scholz: *Ärzte und Patienten in Dresdner Natur-heilsanatorien.* medizin-bibliothek-information 4 (2004) Nr. 1, p. 13.

A sort of light-air-Goddess promotes the amenities of the prestigious "Bilz Sanatorium" in Radebeul near Dresden (Saxony).

▷ Chap. 2: The "New Man" ◁

The Beaming Human

Cosmic energy within the organism

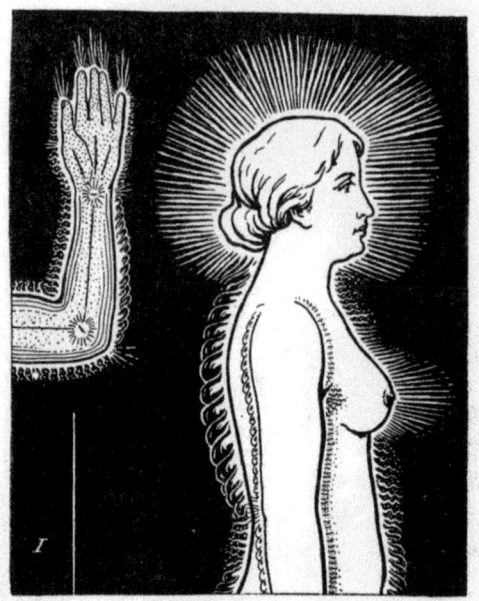

Der strahlende Mensch.

Die gebogenen Strahlen sind magnetische, die kurzen kleinen, odische, die flammigen Wärme- und die längsten die Helioda- oder geistige Lebensstrahlen. Der Charakter der verschiedenen Strahlen ist von Carl Huter zum ersten Male experimentell festgestellt worden.

Carl Huter: *Illustriertes Handbuch der praktischen Menschenkenntnis nach meinem System der wissenschaftlichen Psycho-Physiognomik Körper-, Kopf-. Gesichts- u. Augenausdruckskunde.* 3rd edition. Leipzig, 1928, p. 32.

The esoteric freelancer Carl Huter (1861-1912) combined mesmeric, physiognomic, and religious ideas. He defined the "Helioda beams" as "spiritual life beams".

▷ Chap. 2: The "New Man" ◁

In the "temple of nature"

Science as a sort of religion

FRONTISPIECE.

THE TEMPLE OF NATURE

Erasmus Darwin: *The Temple of Nature or the Origin of Society; a poem.* London, 1803: frontispiece (by Johann Heinrich Füssli).

The grandfather of Charles Darwin praises in this didactic poem the creativity of Nature anticipating the evolution theory of is grandson. Unveiling the Goddess Nature (Isis) was then a common metaphor for naturalists.

▷ Chap 2: "Temple of Nature" ◁

Natural science referring to divine nature

Helmholtz leaning onto an Artemis (Isis) herm

Monument at the Humboldt University in Berlin (Photo: H. Schott, 2014)

The monument was erected 1899 in reference to ancient mythology.

▷ Chap 2: "Temple of Nature" ◁

A Savant Unveiling Nature

Natura depicted as a many-breasted goddess

From F. Peyrard: *De la Nature et de ses lois*. Paris, 1793.

A very popular motif in the discourse of natural science about 1800.

▷ Chap 2: "Temple of Nature" ◁

Idol of the "German mother"

Religious implications of the Nazi propaganda

Poster by Joachim Schich (1937), supporting the National Socialist *"Hilfswerk Mutter und Kind"* (Aid Organization Mother and Child).

The "German mother" like a Madonna with baby Jesus and a sunlike halo was an ideal counter-image of the degenerated, inferior, and ugly "sub-human beings" (*Untermenschen*).

▷ Chap. 2: Degenerated Nature ◁

Nature and technique: corresponding magicians

Technical innovations as natural magic

Julius Zöllner: *Die Kräfte der Natur und ihre Benutzung. Eine physikalische Technologie*. 7th ed. Leipzig, 1877: frontispiece.

▷ Chap. 2: Second Nature ◁

Technical device in the form of a nature goddess

Extinguishing the firebug (*Feuerteufel*)

Julius Zöllner: *Die Kräfte der Natur und ihre Benutzung. Eine physikalische Technologie.* 7th ed. Leipzig, 1877, p. 167.

The image corresponds to the chapter on hydraulic machines, pumps, and fire pumps. The motto quotes verses by Goethe, whose poetical observation of nature was still popular then. The woman with her right arm, formed as a water hose, symbolizes the power of the natural element water driven by a pump.

▷ Chap. 2: Second Nature ◁

The Queens of Telegraphy

Two women symbolize the global communication

Die Erfindung des Telegraphen.

Julius Zöllner: *Die Kräfte der Natur und ihre Benutzung. Eine physikalische Technologie*. 7th ed. Leipzig, 1877, after p. 346.

The symbolic implications of the image are interesting: The black woman symbolizes the Queen of Night (located in the Southern Hemisphere), the white woman above the Queen of Heaven, both female personifications of *Natura* and as such promotors of telegraphy, a revolutionary technical innovation.

▷ Chap. 2: Second Nature ◁

Modern times and technical revolution

Personified by a Joan of Arc-like woman

„Modern Times" (before 1882) by Franz Simm (1853-1918)

Elke Frietsch: *"Kulturproblem Frau". Weiblichkeitsbilder in der Kunst des Nationalsozialismus.* Köln, Weimar; Wien, 2006: Abb. 30.

The graphic shows the triumph of the technical revolution personified by a female figure raising a torch and a telegraph post. She is surrounded by symbols of the technical progress: gearwheel, factory chimney, phial, and wheel rim. On the left side, a triumph column displays the attributes of progress inspired by the Napoleonic era.

▷ Chap. 2: Second Nature ◁

Isis as patroness of animal magnetism

The imagery of the unveiled goddess

ISIS REVELATA:

An Inquiry

INTO

THE ORIGIN, PROGRESS, AND PRESENT STATE

OF

Animal Magnetism:

BY

J. C. COLQUHOUN, ESQ. ADVOCATE,

F.R.S.E.

VOL. II.

EDINBURGH, MACLACHLAN & STEWART,
AND BALDWIN & CRADOCK, LONDON.

John Campbell Colquhoun: *Isis Revelata: an inquiry into the origin, progress, and present state of animal magnetism*. Vol. 2. Edinburgh, 1836: title page.

Statue of the goddess of healing in a sanctuary with a caduceus in her left arm.

▷ Chap. 3: Hypnosis ◁

The hidden truth in a dark cave

The program of scientific enlightenment

Johann Baptist van Helmondt [translation by Christian Knorr von Rosen-roth]: *Aufgang der Artzney-Kunst [...]*. Sulzbach, 1683: frontispiece.

Van Helmont reports a "dream": First Galen, Avicenna, Theophrastus (Paracelsus), and finally van Helmont himself tried to enlighten the "tomb of the truth" (*Grab der Wahrheit*).

▷ Chap. 3: The Unconscious ◁

The healing sleep as a topic of mesmerism

Hypnos is lead away by Aesclepius

Carl Alexander Ferdinand Kluge: *Versuch einer Darstellung des animalischen Magnetismus als Heilmittel.* Berlin 1811: title page (detail).

According to the Greek mythology (Hesiod), Night (i.e. nature) gives birth to the twin brothers *Thanatos* (death) and *Hypnos* (sleep). It is remarkable that Kluge, a surgeon and university professor in Berlin, highlighted *Hypnos* in combination with Asclepius, the Greek healing god, as a therapeutic agent in the sense of animal magnetism (mesmerism) – about 30 years before the terms "hypnosis" and "hypnotism" were coined.

The Night would be the "the creator of all beautiful and horrible, dark and mysterious, being therefore the mother of the brothers sleep and death".

▷ Chap. 3: The Unconscious ◁

Mother Nature casting the evils

The utopian idea of a paradise on earth

MOTHER NATURE CASTING (D) EVILS OUT OF HER CHILDREN.

Andrew Jackson Davis: *Mental disorders; or, Diseases of the Brain and Nerves, developing the origin and philosophy of mania, insanity´, and crime, with full directions for their treatment and cure.* Special Ed. New York, 1871: frontispiece.

The caption declares: "It is only by obedience to the high behests of nature that these evils can be exorcised, and soul and body be restored to the beauty and happiness on earth."

Davis (1826-1910) was an American spiritualist practicing animal magnetism (mesmerism) and had allegedly clairvoyant powers. He published a series of books dealing with religious, occultist topics.

▷ Chap. 3: Spirit and spirits (ghosts) ◁

The healing power of artificial electricity

A panacea against palsy and asthenia of all kinds

Johann Gottlieb Schäffer: *Die Electrische Medicin oder die Kraft und Wirkung der Electricität in dem menschlichen Körpe [...]* [1st edition 1752]. Regensburg, 1766: frontispiece.

Artificial electricity was one of the most important innovations in the era of Enlightenment (18th century). It was taken for a marvelous power, also useful for medical treatment. The illustration shows a Leiden jar, an electrical machine (*Elektrisiermaschine*), and a doctor treating a patient.

▷ Chap. 4: Electricity and magnetism ◁

Electrical performances and wonders

The "electrical bath" of a young lady

Willem van Barneveld: *Medizinische Elektrizität*. Leipzig, 1787: table 1.

The sensational, spectacular phenomena of electricity fascinated scientists as well as laypeople in the second half of the 18th century. They stimulated the concept of animal magnetism founded by Franz Anton Mesmer (1734-1815) about 1775 in Vienna.

▷ Chap. 4: Electricity and magnetism ◁

The "magnetic fire" visualized

Making the invisible *fluidum* visible

Denis Jules Du Potet [de Sennevoy]: *Die entschleierte Magie. Mit einem Porträt des Verfassers und 19 Abbildungen* [French first edition 1852]. 3rd and 4th Ed. Leipzig, 1925: p. 118.

The French magnetizer and esoteric Du Potet (1796-1881) identified « magnetism » with « magic » and launched mesmerism in England. Who intended to produce magical things had to release subtle magnetic rays, which he illustrated with flames. From 1837 to 1845 he practised also as a homeopathic physician in London.

▷ Chap. 4: Mesmerism ◁

"Magnetic rays" rendered visible

A magnetizer transfers the magnetic *fludium* to a young lady

Ebenezer Sibly: *A Key to Physic, and the Occult Sciences [...].* London, 1794.

The image shows the basic idea of animal magnetism (mesmerism): A subtle cosmic energy, the so-called *fludium* visualized as rays coming out of the palms has to be transferred from the magnetizer to the patient's nerves producing the "magnetic sleep", in which state the magnetic manipulations could be accomplished.

▷ Chap. 4: Mesmerism ◁

"Electroculture" in agriculture

Electrically charged water for vitalizing plants

Source: https://alpovni.wordpress.com/tag/electroculture/

The physician l'abbé Pierre Bertholon de Saint-Lazare from Montpellier, a friend of Benjamin Franklin, tried to apply electricity also beyond medicine. So, he suggested in his book *"De l'Électricité des végétaux"* (1783) methods how to treat plants by means of electricity. Even in the early 20th century, large-scale experiments of *"l'électroculture"* were performed in France.

The illustration shows a jet of electrically charged water resembling the rays visualizing the magnetic *fludium* on the previous illustration. In the 1780s, the novel achievement of electricity including galvanism and animal magnetism stimulated scientific and technological experiments.

▷ Chap. 4: Mesmerism ◁

The "magnetic" irradiation for medical purposes

Mesmeric manipulations of a magnetizer

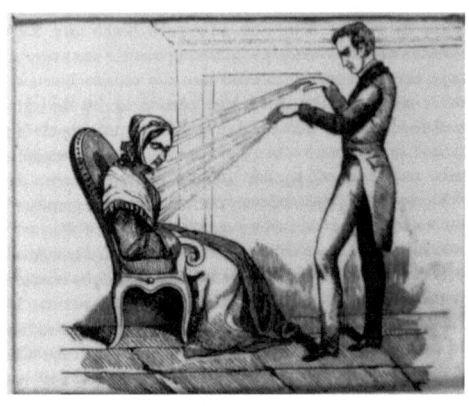

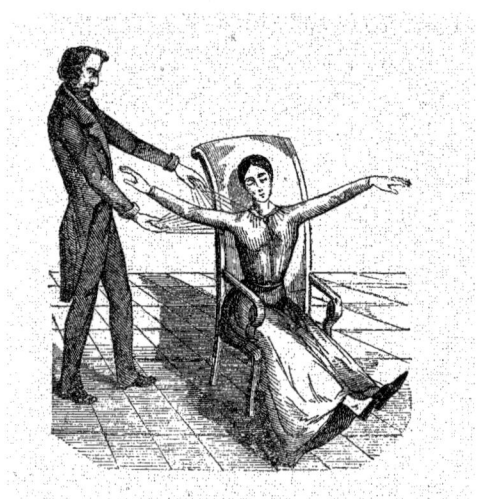

Woodcut (1845): The show magnetizer Charles Lafontaine in action.

http:// images.wellcome.ac.uk/indexplus/image/V0011094ET.html;
http://images.wellcome. ac.uk/indexplus/image/V0011094EB.html

▷ Chap. 4: Mesmerism ◁

Memer's magnetic tub (*baquet*)

Magnetic cure as a group therapy

Baquet, once used by Mesmer (above), today in Lyon (*Musée d'histoire de la Médecine*). In contrast to the original construction suggested by Mesmer, an electrical system (Leiden jar) was here integrated. Mesmer approved this modification, although he always stated that the magnetic *fluidum* was the effective agent, not electricity of magnets.

Mesmer's magnetic cure around the *baquet magnétique*, a very spectacular group therapy in pre-revolutionary Paris, which became a world sensation.

▷ Chap. 4: Mesmerism ◁

The astonishing variety of magnetic tubs

L'homme baquet, a unique construction

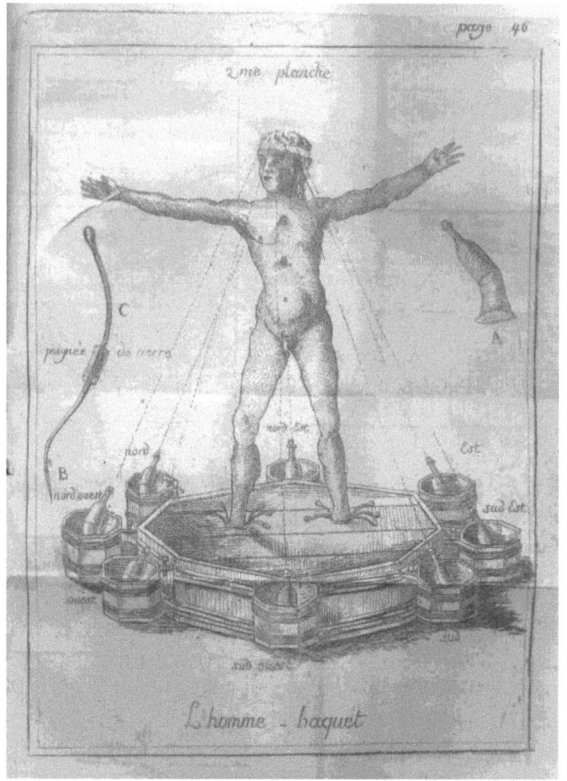

Franz Anton Mesmer: *Correspondance de M. M***** sur les nuovelles dé-couvertes du baquet octogone, de l'homme baquet, det du baquet morale, pouvant servir de suite aux Aphorismes, [...].* Paris, 1785: after p. 46.

Mesmer's followers created different devices and discussed their efficacy sometimes controversially. Regarding this model, the body organs of glass should be magnetically charged through the bottlenecks directed to the head of the model. Patients could derive beneficial *fluidum* from the model by pointing with the iron stick (B,C) to their corresponding ill organ.

▷ Chap. 4: Mesmerism ◁

Divine light through the Eye of God

The well of all the power of nature

Jakob Böhme: *Seraphinisch Blumen-Gärtlein [...].* Amsterdam, 1700: frontispiece.

The image shows a right eye, typical for the iconography of the Eye of God, coalescing with the human eye perceiving God's splendor in a mystical union (*unio mystica*).

Böhme (1575-1624) was a German mystic, philosopher, and theosophist.

▷ Chap. 5: Divine light ◁

Jakob Böhme's vision of Jacob's Ladder

Jakob Böhme: *Mysterium Magnum, Oder Erklärung über das Erste Buch Mosis [...]*. Amsterdam, 1682.

Böhme looking up Jacob's Ladder, where angels descend from and ascend to the divine light on the top. God is symbolized through a radiant triangle.

▷ Chap. 5: Divine light ◁

Jesus and Satan: Light contra darkness

Dangerous, evil, dark nature

[Paul Kaym:] *Helleleuchtender Hertzens-Spiegel [...]*. Amsterdam; Dantzig, 1680: table IV.

"*Gratia*" (sun, God) and "*Natura*" (moon, evil) send their rays into a heart in the form of two combined bottles with separate necks and openings. The contrast between good and evil is evident.

▷ Chap. 5: Divine light ◁

Divine and diabolic suggestions

In the view of early modern theosophy

[Paul Kaym:] *Hellerleuchtender Hertzens-Spiegel [...].* Amsterdam; Dantzig,
1680: table I.

The human heart in the form of a face is filled with divine wisdom. The Word
of God is blown into the right ear, devil's word into the left.

▷ Chap. 5: Dark demons ◁

The microcosm embedded in a cosmic harmony

The human body traversed by a vertical string

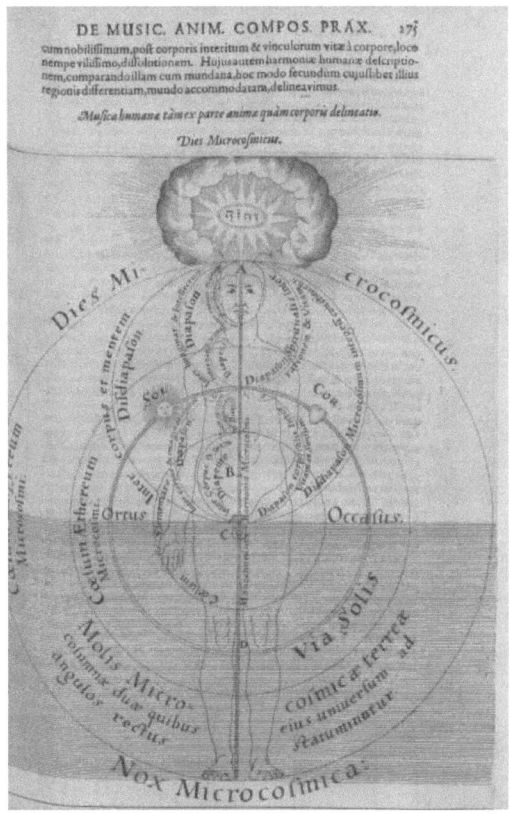

Robert Fludd: *Utriusque Cosmi [...]*. Tomus secundus. Tractatus Primus. Oppenheim, 1619: p. 275.

The string (*Monochordium Harmoniae Microcosmi*) links the microcosm with God, so its life spirits are connected with the world spirit. The "music of the spheres" played an interesting role in early modern anthropology.

▷ *Effluvia*: Magical outflow ◁

Allegory of music reminding of *Natura*

An erudite, creative, majestic lady

Jean Baptiste Boudard: *Iconologie tirée de divers auteurs. Ouvrage utile aux gens de lettres [...].* Wien, 1766 : p. 218.

In 1759, Boudard published his *Iconologie* in three volumes including 630 etchings with a series of female figures symbolizing knowledge and skill.

▷ *Effluvia*: Magical outflow ◁

Art and Nature cooperating in practice

Two female figures represent alchemical art and natural magic

Johann Nicolas Martius: *Unterricht von der Magia Naturali Und derselben Medicinischen Gebrauch auf Magische Weise [...].* Frankfurt; Leipzig, 1724: frontispiece.

Ars, traditionally of female sex, resembles her Hermes or Mercury.

▷ Chap. 5: Signatures ◁

The Physiognomy reveals the character

Plato as a "sleuth"

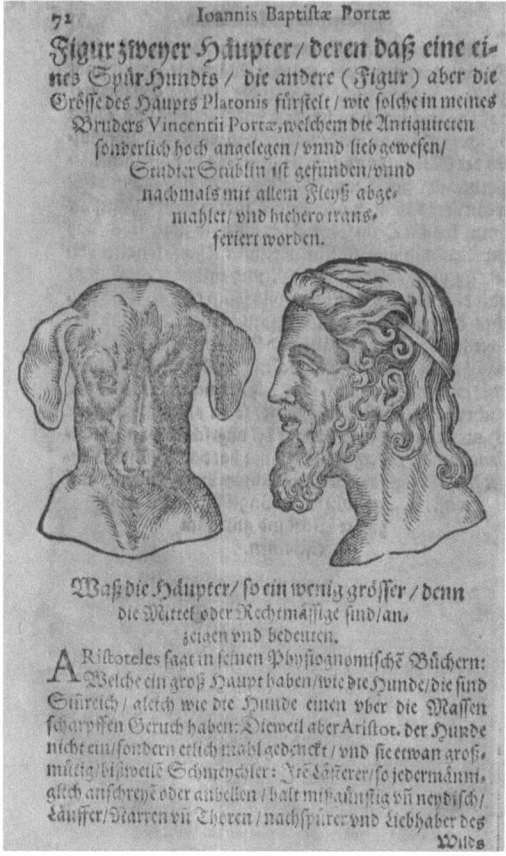

Giambattista Della Porta: *Menschliche Physiognomy [...].* Frankfurt am Main, 1601 [*De humana Physiognomonia;* German]: p. 72.

Della Porta referring Aristotle stated that those, who had a large head size like the depicted dog, would be ingenious.

▷ Chap. 5: Signatures ◁

Signatures point to the hidden (healing) powers

The roots of orchids raise virility and fertility

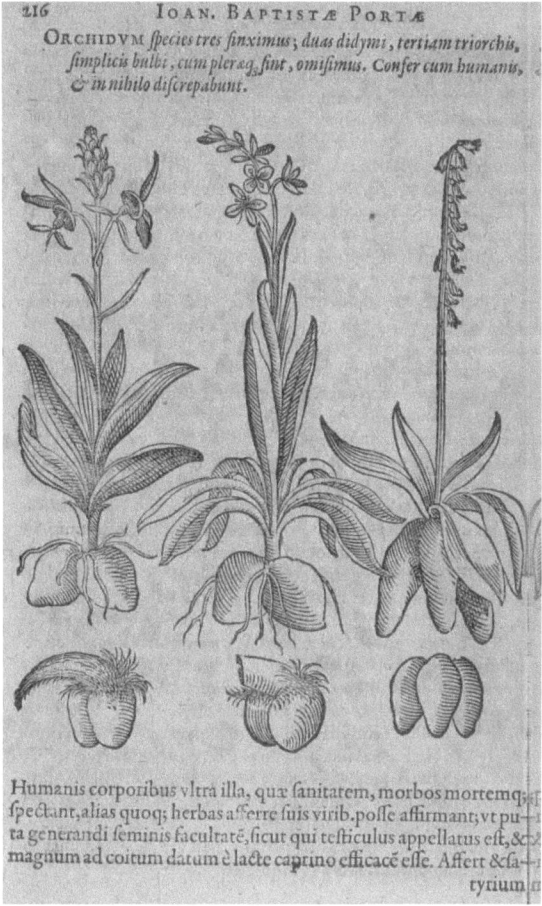

216   IOAN. BAPTISTÆ PORTÆ

ORCHIDVM *species tres finximus; duas didymi, tertiam triorchis, simplicis bulbi, cum pleræq, fint, omisimus. Confer cum humanis, & in nihilo discrepabunt.*

Humanis corporibus vltrà illa, quæ fanitatem, morbos mortemq; fpectant, alias quoq; herbas afferre fuis virib.poffe affirmant; vt puta generandi feminis facultaté,ficut qui tefticulus appellatus eft,& magnum ad coitum datum è lacte caprino efficacé effe. Affert &fa-
tyrium

Giambattista Della Porta: *Phytognomonica. [...]* Frankfurt, 1608. The writings of the Italian savant Della Porta (1535-1615) were very influential.

The testicle-like roots were traditionally used as aphrodisiacs.

▷ Chap. 5: Signatures ◁

Jacob's Ladder in the Middle Ages

The ascend of men fighting against demons

The *Ladder of Divine Ascent*: icon (12ᵗʰ c.) according to a manuscript of the monk John Climacus (Saint Catherine's Monastery, Mount Sinai, Egypt).

John Climacus is shown on the top of the ladder welcomed by Jesus. The spectacle is observed by a group of saints (above) and a group of venerable men on the bottom.

▷ Chap. 5: *Arcanum* ◁

Jacob's ladder of the natural philosophers

Symbol of the early modern natural science

Robert Fludd: *Utriusque Cosmi [...]*. Tomus secundus. Tractatus Primus. Oppenheim, 1619: p. 272.

The ascend on the ladder corresponded to the contemporary alchemical idea to perform a process of material *and* spiritual purification. It should lead likeweise to real knowledge and divine wisdom. The rungs of the ladder were named (ascending): *Sensus – Imaginatio – Ratio – Intellectus – Intelligentia – Verbum*. The Word of God (*verbum*) was the last rung next to the light of God.

▷ Chap. 5: *Arcanum* ◁

Early modern natural science

Johann Michael Fehr*: Anchora sacra; vel scorzonera*. Jena, 1666: title copper.

Fehr (1610-1688), a co-founder of the *Academia Naturae Curiosorum* (later: *Leopoldina*), presents here his monograph on the black salsify.

▷ Chap. 5: *Arcanum* ◁

Erotic symbolism of the alchemical thinking

The copulation of sun and moon in a water bath

EMBLEMA XXXIV. *De secretis Naturæ.* 145
In balneis concipitur,& in aëre nascitur,rubeus verò
factus graditur super aquas.

EPIGRAMMA XXXIV.

B *Alnea conceptu pueri,natalibus aër*
Splendet & hinc rubeus sub pede cernit aquas.
Fitque super montana cacumina candidus ille,
Qui remanet doctis unica cura viris.
Est lapis & non est,cœli quod nobile Donum,
Dante D E O fœlix,si quis habebit,erit. T Ho-

Michael Maier: *Chymisches Cabinet/ Drer grossen Geheimnussen der Natur* […] Frankfurt, 1708 [= *Atalanta fugiens* (1618); German]: p. 145, Emblem 34. Copper engraving by Matthäus Merian.

The German physician and learned alchemist Michael Maier (1568-1622) was involved in the Rosicrucean movement. This emblem illustrates the alchemical *coniunctio*, the copulation of gold (sun) and silver (moon), an example of the "chemical marriage" or "chymical wedding".

▷ Chap. 5: "Chymical wedding" ◁

Copulation as a moment of the alchemical process

The unification of sun and moon (*Sol & Luna*)

Rosarium Philosophorum (Rosary of the Philosophers). The fifth out of twenty woodcuts shows the "chymical wedding". Sun and moon, gold and silver, king and queen are imagined as analogous couples.

The "Rosary" is a 16th century alchemical tract published in 1550 in Frankfurt. The very popular psychological interpretation of the symbols of alchemy by C. G. Jung in the 20th century was criticized by historians of science for neglecting the context of the contemporary natural history and technique.

▷ Chap. 5: "Chymical wedding" ◁

Goddess Nature as a young lady

The Egyptian Isis as a shining example

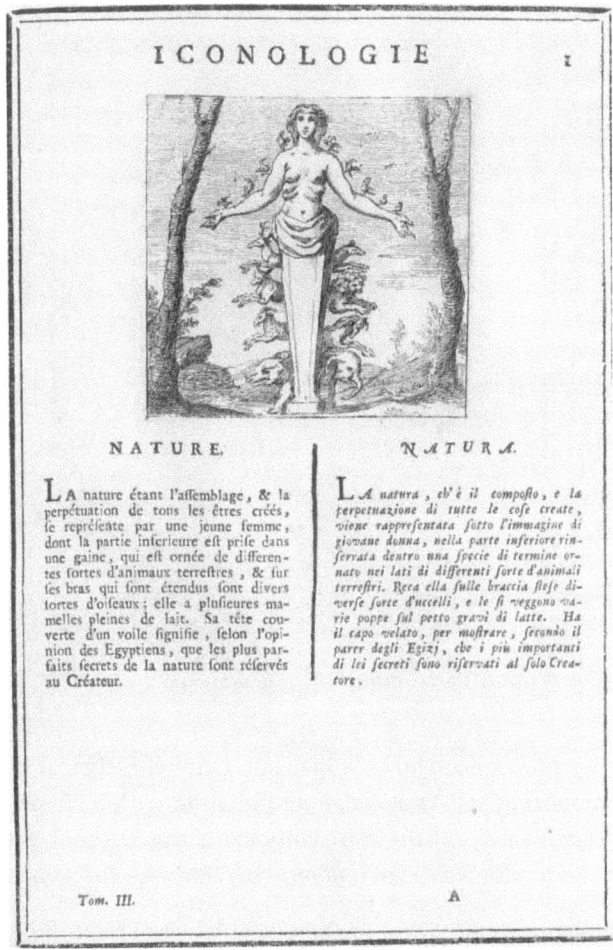

Jean Baptiste Boudard: *Iconologie tirée de divers auteurs* [...]. Vienna, 1766: table 1.

▷ Chap. 6: Goddess *Natura* ◁

The personification of "Science"

Science is female like Nature

Jean Baptiste Boudard: *Iconologie tirée de divers auteurs* [...]. Parma, 1759.

This allegory of Science shows a majestic lady with typical attributes: a mirror symbolizing self-knowledge and a globe with a "female" triangle (pointing downward) on the top symbolizing the element water, which can also be understood as a goniometer characteristic for an architect.

The personified Science reminds of respective representations of Nature. In the view of early modern scholars, the primary scientist was nature, which had to be investigated and imitated by human scientists.

▷ Chap. 6: Goddess *Natura* ◁

Divine Nature as a guide for human scholars

One has to follow her footprints

EMBLEMA XLII. *De secretis Naturæ.* 177

In Chymicis verſanti Natura, Ratio, Experientia & lectio,
ſint Dux, ſcipio, perſpicilia & lampas.

EPIGRAMMA XLII.

DUx Natura tibi, túque arte pediſſequus illi
Eſto lubens, erras, ni comes ipſa viæ eſt,
Det ratio ſcipionis opem, Experientia firmet
Lumina, quò poſſit cernere poſta procul.
Lectio ſit lampas tenebris dilucida, rerum
Verborúmque ſtrues providus ut caveas. Z CAS-

Michael Maier: *Atalanta fugiens, hoc est, Emblemata nova de secretis naturae chymica [...].* Oppenheim, 1618: p. 117.

This emblem shows symbolically the instruments of the adept of Nature: stick (i.e. reason), lantern (i.e. light for reading), and glasses (i.e. experience, reading).

▷ Chap. 6: Goddess *Natura* ◁

Natura linking heaven and earth, God and man

Nature as a divine medium for men of science

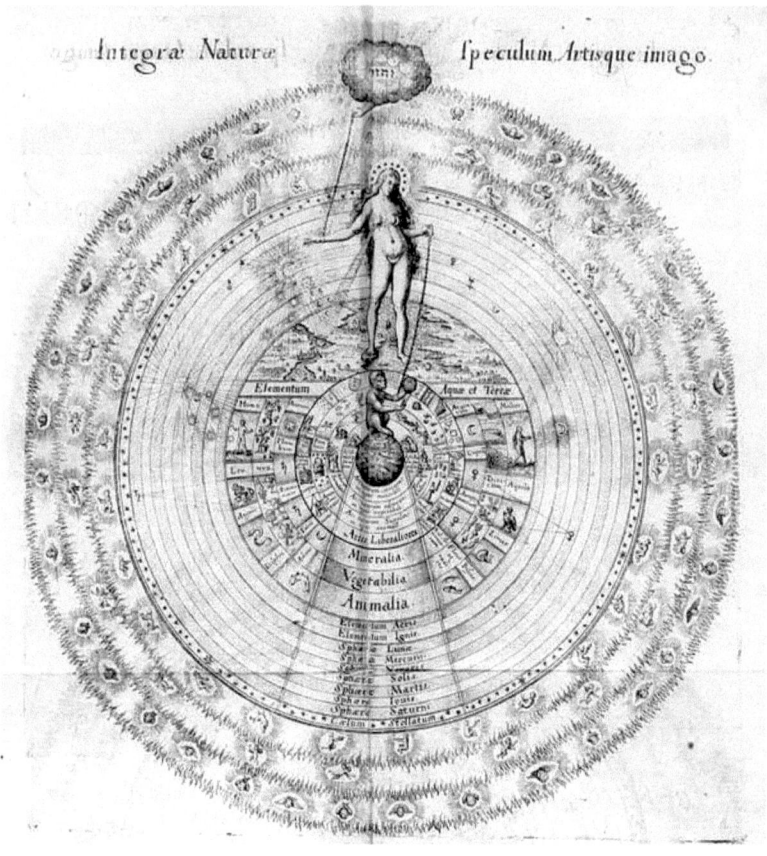

Robert Fludd,: *Utriusque Cosmi* [...]. Tomus primus. Oppenheim, 1617.

A sort of Golden Chain goes out from the hand of God and *Natura* hands it down to the ape (i.e. the scholar) on the globe.

▷ Chap. 6: Goddess *Natura* ◁

Nature as a female blacksmith

Creator in the service of God

Illustrations of the *Roman de la Rose* (authored in the 13th century).

Nature in her forge (above): French manuscript; Nature creating the "new man" (below), woodcut from a printed edition (Lyon, about 1487).

▷ Chap. 6: Goddess *Natura* ◁

Witchcraft and black magic

"*Hexenschuss*", a painful attack

Woodcut from Ulrich Molitor: *Hexen Meyeterey*. Constance, 1545.

A witch attacks a man producing lumbago (*Hexenschuss* in German). The witch-hunt culminated not in the Middle Ages, but in the very early modern period.

▷ Chap. 6: Devil, witches, and evil spiritis ◁

Promoters of Enlightenment fight against demonology

Caricature of the witch-hunt

Christian Thomasius: *Kurtze Lehr-Sätze Von dem Laster der Zauberey*. Aus dem Lateinischen ins Teutsche übersetzet. 1706: frontispiece.

The well-known jurist and philosopher Thomasius (1655-1728) blamed the witch-hunt and the common use of torture. The image ridicules the popular superstitions still alive at that time.

▷ Chap. 6: Devil, witches, and evil spirits ◁

Nature as a master of the alchemist

The alchemy of nature personified as a crowned angel

Miniature illustrating Jean Perréal's poem *"La complainte de nature à l'alchimist errant"* (1516).

Nature invites the alchemist to leave his forge and come over to hers, symbolized by the tree with its roots *Mineralia*, *Vegetabilia*, and *Sensitiva* (inscriptions are hardly to read) with vegetal gold on the top.

▷ Chap. 6: Controversial images of women ◁

Blending of central female figures in the Renaissance

Eve driven out of paradise resembling Mary and *Natura*

Woodcut from Jacopo Filippo Foresti: *De plurimis clairs selecitsque muli-eribus.* Ferrara, 1497.

Eve does not look like a sinner at all. She rather resembles a nurturing mother in a convenient natural environment. One can interpret the figure as a personification of nature, blended with Godmother Mary (together with Jesus and John).

▷ Chap. 6: Mary – *Natura* ◁

Divine wisdom (*Sophia*) like a queen

Manifestations of Natura

Above: Woodcut from Jacopo Filippo Foresti: *De plurimis clairs selecitsque mulieribus.* Ferrara, 1497: The legendary Pope Joan.

Below: *Philosophia*; woodcut by Albrecht Dürer (1502)

▷ Chap. 6: Mary – *Natura* ◁

The Queen of Heaven as Alma Mater

Sophia nourishing the Seven Liberal Arts

Drawing (12th century) from Thomas Schipflinger: *Sophia – Maria. Eine ganzheitliche Vision der Schöpfung [...].* München; Zürich, 1988, p. 238.

Sophia inspires the seven liberal arts (grammar, rhetoric, dialectic, arithmetic, geometry, music, astronomy) – all of them female.

▷ Chap. 6: Mary – *Natura* ◁

Virgin of Mercy (*Schutzmantelmadonna*)

Mary, the divine helper of humans

Wilhelm Gumppenberg: *Atlas marianus sive Imaginibus Deiparae Per Orbem Christinum Miraculsis.* 2nd ed. Ingolstadt, 1659, after p. 69.

Virgin of Mercy from the *Basilica di S. Maria di Monte Berico* (Vicenza).

The Bavarian Jesuit Gumppenberg (1609-1675) recorded ca. 1200 locations of Marian devotion.

▷ Chap. 6: Mary – *Natura* ◁

Mary with Jacob's ladder

Symbolizing the ascend to divine wisdom

Wilhelm Gumppenberg: *Atlas marianus sive Imaginibus Deiparae Per Orbem Christinum Miraculsis.* 2nd ed. Ingolstadt, 1659, after p. 144.

The *"Madona de Scala Messanae"* reminds of Jacob's ladder, also used by "philosophers" highlighting the progress of scientific enlightenment.

▷ Chap. 6: Mary – *Natura* ◁

Mother Earth as a wet nurse

The "matrix" was conceived as a cosmic uterus

Michael Maier: *Atalanta fugiens [...].* Oppenheim, 1618, p. 17.

The emblem demonstrates the view of early modern natural philosophers – as Paracelsus put it: The "whole woman", the *matrix*, would be the earth and all the elements.

▷ Chap. 6: *Matrix*, motherly Nature ◁

Jesus Christ within earthly Mary and cosmic Sophia

Nature pregnant with God's marvels

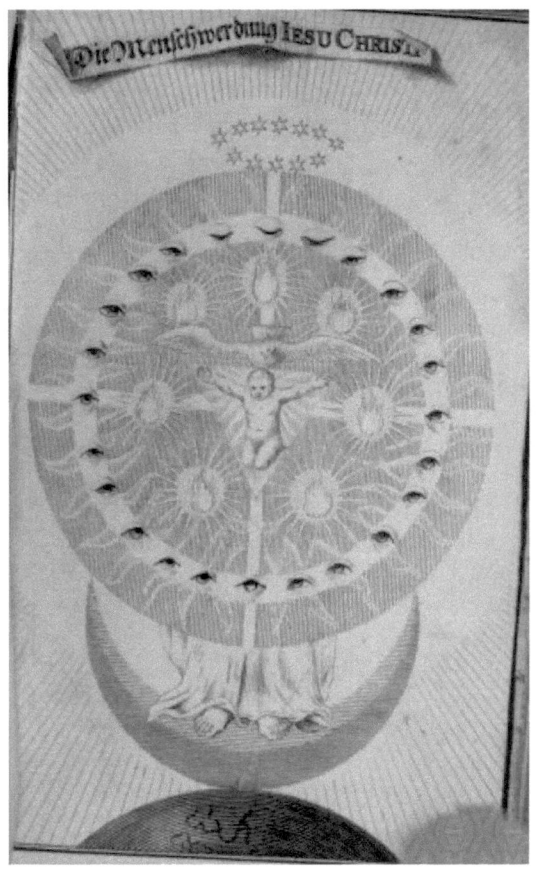

Jakob Böhme: *Von der Menschwerdung Jesu Christi [...]*. Amsterdam, 1682: frontispiece.

Virgin Mary standing on the crescent is concealed by a fiery circle with divine eyes symbolizing Sophia. In the center Jesus Christ in a uterus-like triangle.

▷ Chap. 6: *Matrix*, motherly Nature ◁

Romantic anthropology

"Day life" and "night life", a circular model

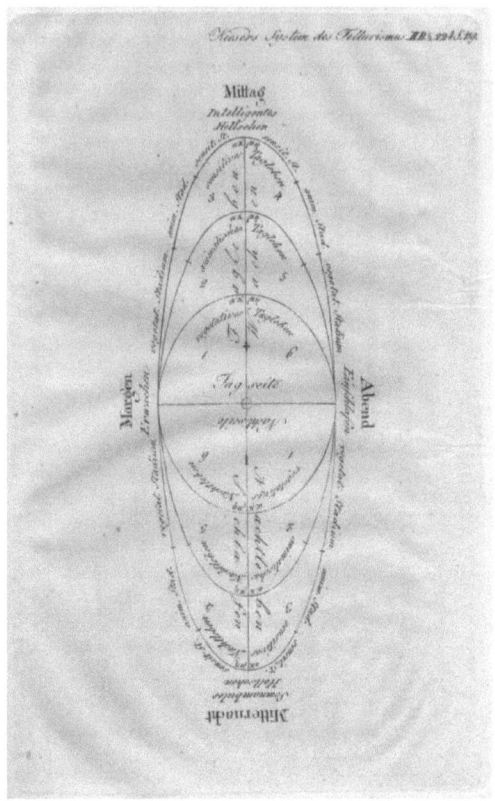

Dietrich Georg Kieser: *System des Tellurismus oder Thierischen Magnetismus. Ein Handbuch für Naturforscher und Ärzte.* New Edition. Leipzig, 1826: vol. 2, after p. 118.

„Dayside" (*Tagseite*) and „nightside" (*Nachtseite*) of the psychic life in between „intelligent clairvoyance" and "somnambulist clairvoyance" as turning points.

▷ Chap. 6: Luna, the Moon ◁

Science (*Scientia*) in view of Nature (*Natura*)

Visualized as female savant

Anleitung zur primitiven gabalistischen Wissenschaft, und zur symbolischen Zahlenkenntniß für alle Sprachen anwendbar [ca. 1790]: frontispiece.

The frontispiece of this cabalistic textbook shows a woman looking up to heaven with a crescent and an arc of stars. Obviously, she is reflecting the mysteries of mathematics, the top discipline of science.

▷ Chap. 6: *Luna*, the Moon ◁

What does this woman represent?

Albrecht Dürer's *"Melencolia I"* reconsidered

Copper engraving by Albrecht Dürer (1514).

This famous image has been interpreted very differently, mostly in association with "melancholy". But the title *Melencolia* may be misleading. Is the winged woman rather an incarnation of divine science reflecting the mysteries of the magic of nature as the comet in the sky indicates?

▷ Chap. 6: *Luna*, the Moon ◁

An emblem on moon (*luna*) and fortune (*fortuna*)

Nature-like goddess of the sublunary world

George Wither: *A Collection of Emblems, ancient and modern*. Books 1-4. London, 1634- 1635; book 3: p. 174.

Wither (1588-1667) was an English poet and satirist. In this emblem he links fortune with the moon in different ways (veil in a moon-like form, crescent in one hand). The message is: Fortune changes like the moon. Her shock of hair is probably an allusion to the ancient figure of *Kairos*.

▷ Chap. 6: *Luna*, the Moon ◁

Ecstasis, enlightenment, orgasm (?)

Saint Teresa of Ávila as an example par excellence

Source: http://en.wikipedia.org/wiki/File:Teresabernini.JPG

"The Ecstasy of Saint Teresa" (*L'Estasi di Santa Teresa*) designed and completed in 1652 by Gian Lorenzo Bernini; central sculptural group in white marble in the church *Santa Maria della Vittoria* in Rome.

Saint Teresa of Ávila (1515–1582), was a roman Catholic saint and famous Spanish mystic.

Bernini's artistic depiction of Teresa's mystical experience implies erotic and even sexual moments.

▷ Chap. 7: Love and Mysticism ◁

Onanism, the source of all evil
"Self-abuse" as the ultimate sin

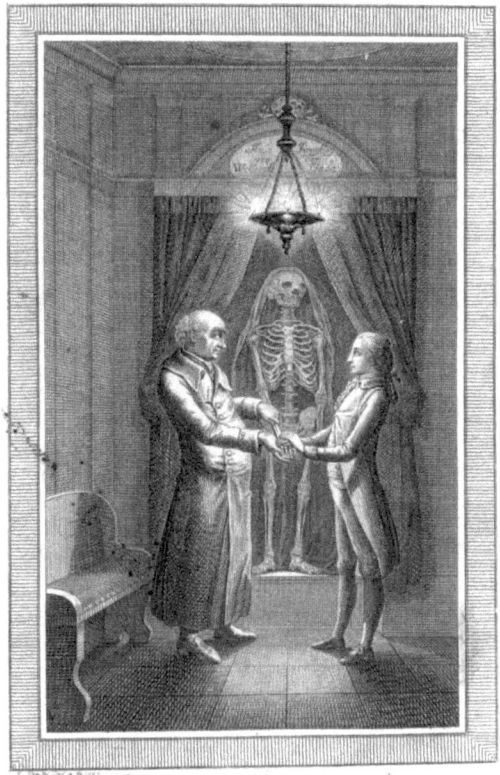

Wenn schnöde Wollust dich erfüllt,
So werde durch dies Schreckenbild,
Verdorter Todenknochen,
Der Kitzel unterbrochen.

Gotthilf Sebastian Rötger: *Über Kinderunzucht und Selbstbefleckung. Ein Buch bloß für Ältern, Erzieher und Jugendfreunde.* Züllichau, 1787: frontispiece.

The vow of a young man against onanism in front of a skeleton.

▷ Chap. 7: Sexuality ◁

The extravagant lifestyle of the French nobility

Sexual libertinage and pornography about 1800

Andréa de Nerciat: *Le diable au corps.* Oevre posthume (1803). Vol. 1 : frontispiece.

In his pornographic work in 3 volumes, the French novelist de Nerciat (1749-1800) describes, how a Marquise is licked (*gamahucher*) by her lap dog every day.

▷ Chap. 7: Sexuality ◁

Bridal mysticism in Christian tradition

Bridegroom (Christ) and bride (soul) decorate the wedding bed

Simon Huebmann: *Geistliches Bräut-Bethlein, mit Blumen bestreut* [...]. Salzburg, 1669: frontispiece.

Bridal mysticism was still quite popular in the 18th century.

▷ Chap. 7: Holy Marriage ◁

The Holy Marriage performed on earth

The spectacular "Celestial Bed" in London in the 1780s

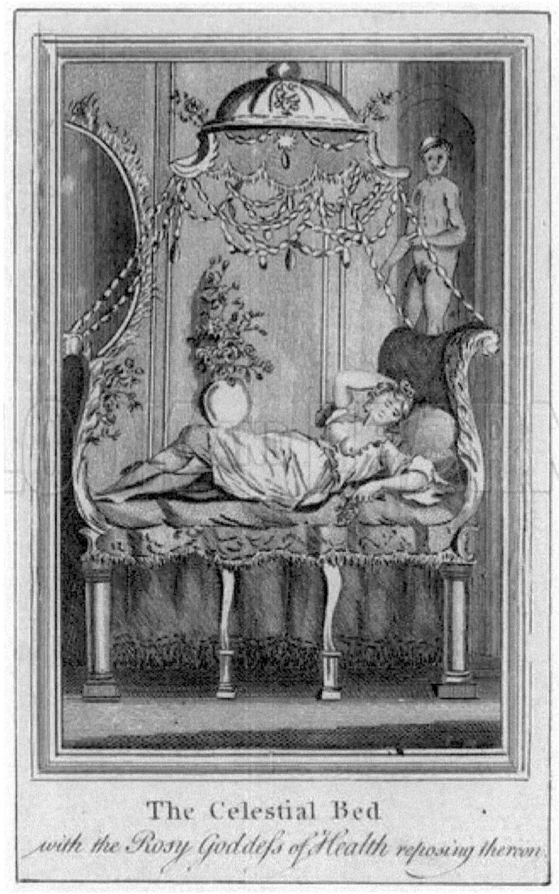

The Celestial Bed
with the Rosy Goddefs of Health reposing thereon

James Graham: *The Celestial Beds [...].* London, 1781.

Graham (1745-1794), a "quack" doctor, offered in his *Temple of Health and Hymen* a sort of sexual therapy through his technically refined "Celestial Bed". The later Lady Hamilton played the role of a goddess of health.

▷ Chap. 7: Holy Marriage ◁

The semblance of a Holy Marriage

LES JOIES

CÉLESTES

Fin de la Premiere Partie

John Cleland: *Nouvelle Traduction de Woman of Pleasur ou Fille des Joye de M. Cleland Contenant Les Mémoires de M.elle Fanny.* London: 1776.

▷ Chap. 7: Holy Marriage ◁

Sexual topics in libertine French literature

A mixture of pagan orgy and worship service

Charles Borde(s): *Parapilla, poëme en cinq chants.* Lyon, 1776: title page (detail).

Naked women celebrate the Holy Marriage of Phallus and Hymen (in form of a garland). A scenery before today's term "pornography" was coined.

▷ Chap. 7: Holy Marriage ◁

Intercourse evaluated by excitement curves

The "normal orgasm curve" as the biologistic golden standard

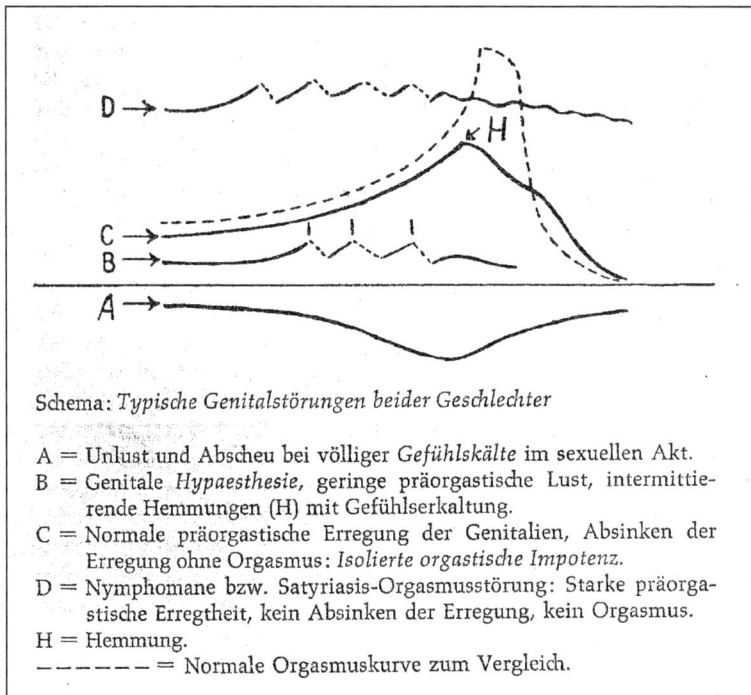

Schema: *Typische Genitalstörungen beider Geschlechter*

A = Unlust und Abscheu bei völliger *Gefühlskälte* im sexuellen Akt.

B = Genitale *Hypaesthesie*, geringe präorgastische Lust, intermittierende Hemmungen (H) mit Gefühlserkaltung.

C = Normale präorgastische Erregung der Genitalien, Absinken der Erregung ohne Orgasmus: *Isolierte orgastische Impotenz.*

D = Nymphomane bzw. Satyriasis-Orgasmusstörung: Starke präorgastische Erregtheit, kein Absinken der Erregung, kein Orgasmus.

H = Hemmung.

— — — — — — = Normale Orgasmuskurve zum Vergleich.

Wilhelm Reich: *Die Funktion des Orgasmus. Sexualökonomische Grundprobleme der biologischen Energie.* Köln, 1969 [Original Edition 1942]: p. 143.

The Austrian medical doctor and psychoanalyst Reich (1897-1957) claimed a radical sexual emancipation and tried to combine Freudian and Marxist ideas. But he became very isolated in both fields. Because of the Nazis he had to emigrate to the US in 1939. His restricting theory of the "orgasm reflex" reveals a crude biologistic anthropology, which was the basis for his specific methods of sexual therapy.

▷ Chap. 7: Sexual revolution ◁

"Sexual magic" and ethnic (*völkisch*) ideology

Esotericism in the early 20ᵗʰ century

Book illustration by Fidus in G. Herman: *Xenologie des Saeming. Neuaus-gabe der „Sexual-Magie".* Leipzig, 1905: after p. xviii.

Sexual magic was partly propagated as a means of race hygiene and human breeding, so that there was an affinity to certain Nazi ideas.

▷ Chap. 7: Erotic magic ◁

The blending of sexuality and spirituality in India

An example for the long tradition of religious eroticism

Jean Varenne: *Le Tantrisme. La sexualité transcendée*. Paris, 1977: frontis-piece [image source untraceable].

Sculpture (10th c.) from the *Kandariya Mahadeva Temple* in *Khajuraho* (India). A man beneath a goddess-like woman.

▷ Chap. 7: Erotic magic ◁

Suggestion – Zauberformel der Entzauberung

Fluidum – Heilkunde der Sympathie

Magia naturalis – Natur als Magierin

Natura – Pendant zu Maria

Eros – Liebeszauber zwischen Sex und Mystik

Epilog
„... wo ächte Götterbilder stehn sollten"

CORRESPONDING HEINZ SCHOTT BLOGS:

Magic of Nature
https://heinzschott.wordpress.com/

Magic of Nature – Supplementary News
https://heinzgustavdotcom2.wordpress.com/

Cover of Part 1

Cover of Part 2

BoD – Books on Demand by the same author in 2017

Himmel oder Hölle. Ansichten zur menschlichen Sexualität

Paperback, 244 pages

ISBN-13: 9783837006018

[SCHOTT's NEUE BIBLIOTHEK /1]

Fluidum. Magische Momente des Mesmerismus

Paperback, 148 pages

ISBN-13: 9783744802055

SCHOTT's NEUE BIBLIOTHEK /2

Karezza. Ethics of Marriage

By Alice B. Stockham.

Edited by Heinz Schott

Paperback, 72 Seiten

ISBN-13: 9783744815086

SCHOTT's NEUE BIBLIOTHEK /3